WHICH JESUS?

WHICH JESUS?

by John Wick Bowman

THE WESTMINSTER PRESS · PHILADELPHIA

ISBN 0-664-24879-9

LIBRARY OF CONGRESS CATALOG CARD NO. 74-100953

PUBLISHED BY THE WESTMINSTER PRESS®
PHILADELPHIA, PENNSYLVANIA

PRINTED IN THE UNITED STATES OF AMERICA

To thirty-five hundred
theological and university students
to whom I owe much and have, I hope,
contributed a little

Contents

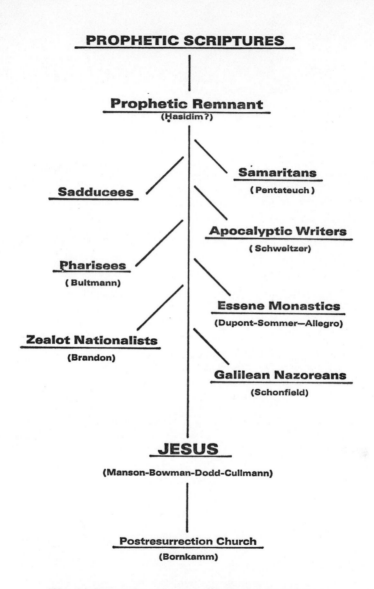

PROPHETIC SCRIPTURES

|

Prophetic Remnant
(Hasidim?)

Samaritans
(Pentateuch)

Sadducees

Apocalyptic Writers
(Schweitzer)

Pharisees
(Bultmann)

Essene Monastics
(Dupont-Sommer—Allegro)

Zealot Nationalists
(Brandon)

Galilean Nazoreans
(Schonfield)

JESUS
(Manson-Bowman-Dodd-Cullmann)

Postresurrection Church
(Bornkamm)

The Hebrew Prophetic—Christian Tradition

Preface

This book has grown out of a series of informal talks given at my Bible Tête-à-tête for lay adults in the United Church of Sun City, Arizona. Its general aim is to assist the layman—and this, of course, includes the university and seminary student—as well as the busy parish minister, to follow the development of scholarly thought about Jesus during the nearly three quarters of a century since nineteen hundred. The date (1900) is crucial since it marks the height of dominance of the "Old Liberal" school of thought in both Biblical and theological circles.

During the intervening years, despite expansive blurbs on paper jackets, few more than a half-dozen distinctive views of an original sort about Jesus have appeared. It is this book's function to present these clearly, marking their likenesses and differences, to indicate the sources upon which their authors have drawn in creating the images of Jesus to which they severally subscribe, and to assist the reader in making a personal appraisal of their views.

The writer is of the opinion that footnotes are an abomination to the layman and that the scholar does not need them. Only the student and pastor are in real need of citations. To serve these latter, a list of books cited or quoted in the text, together with a series of abbreviations referring

to the same, is included. Throughout the book, these abbreviations, followed by relevant page numbers will be
found.

J. W. B.

Sun City, Arizona

Abbreviations

Allegro, J. M.
    ADSS—*The Dead Sea Scrolls* (1958). Penguin Books, Inc.
    ASOC—*The Dead Sea Scrolls and the Origins of Christianity* (1957). Criterion Books, Inc.

Bornkamm, Günther
    BJN—*Jesus of Nazareth,* tr. by Irene and Fraser McLuskey with James M. Robinson (1960). Harper & Row, Publishers, Inc.

Bowman, John Wick
    BIJ—*The Intention of Jesus* (1943). The Westminster Press.
    BRM—*The Religion of Maturity* (1948). Abingdon-Cokesbury Press.

Brandon, S. G. F.
    BJZ—*Jesus and the Zealots* (1967). Charles Scribner's Sons.

Bultmann, Rudolf
    BHST—*The History of the Synoptic Tradition,* tr. by John Marsh from 3d German ed. (1963). Harper & Row, Publishers, Inc.

BJCM—*Jesus Christ and Mythology* (1958). Charles Scribner's Sons.

BJW—*Jesus and the Word* (1934). Charles Scribner's Sons.

BKM—*Kerygma and Myth,* ed. by Hans Werner Bartsch; tr. by R. H. Fuller (1953). London: S.P.C.K.

BNTTh—*The Theology of the New Testament* (2 vols., 1951 and 1955; references are to Vol. I only), tr. by Kendrick Grobel. Charles Scribner's Sons.

BPE—*The Presence of Eternity* (1957). Harper & Brothers.

Cross, Frank M., Jr.
CALQ—*The Ancient Library of Qumran* (rev. ed. 1961). Doubleday & Company, Inc.

Dodd, C. H.
DAS—*According to the Scriptures* (1953). Charles Scribner's Sons.

Dupont-Sommer, A.
DJSQ—*The Jewish Sect of Qumran and the Essenes,* tr. by R. D. Barnett (2d ed., 1955). London: Vallentine, Mitchell & Co., Ltd.

Kümmel, W. G.
KPF—*Promise and Fulfilment,* tr. by Dorothea M. Barton (1957). London: SCM Press, Ltd.

Manson, William
MJM—*Jesus the Messiah* (1946). The Westminster Press.

McCown, C. C.
    MSRJ—*The Search for the Real Jesus* (1940). Charles
        Scribner's Sons.

Peake's Commentary on the Bible
    PCB—ed. by Matthew Black and H. H. Rowley (1960).
        Thomas Nelson & Sons.

Schonfield, Hugh J.
    SPP—*The Passover Plot* (1966). Random House, Inc.

Schweitzer, Albert
    SQ—*The Quest of the Historical Jesus,* tr. by W. Mont-
        gomery (1948). The Macmillan Company.

References to the above books are indicated by the ab-
breviation followed by the page number, thus: BJN-134.

Introduction

The Image of Jesus at the Turn of the Century

Around 1900, two major schools held the field in Biblical and theological studies. These were the school of Comparative Religions (*Religionsgeschichte*) and what today we term the "Old Liberal" school. These schools, both of which were deeply influenced by the scientific discoveries leading to the theory of evolution in its numerous forms, may be said to have merged in their views relative to the so-called "Jesus of history." For, both were one in placing him at a particular point in the development of man, particularly of Oriental man, and precisely of Jewish man. For both schools, Jesus was a Jewish rabbi, however exceptional or even heretical he may have seemed to his contemporaries to have been.

Within the American Church, the popular reaction to this view of Jesus of Nazareth was almost a generation in maturing. When it did come in the early and middle '20s of the present century, this reaction took the form of Fundamentalism—a popular position as extreme in one direction as the more scholarly positions it opposed had been in another. Neither the "Fundies" nor the "Old Liberals" held the other in very high esteem nor was either ever inclined to learn from the other what he had to teach. For our purposes here, this logomachy between sides equally charged with emotionalism and consequent rancor can make no contribution.

In scholarly circles, as one might well imagine, the reaction toward the work of the two schools mentioned was almost immediate, more judicious and precise. Indeed, just one year after the century's end, Wilhelm Wrede's "The Messianic Secret in the Gospels" (in the German) placed the capstone on the "Old Liberal" position with his thesis that the "Messiah secret" found in the Gospel of Mark was in no sense a product of the mind of the historic Jesus, but rather of the church. But on the very day that Wrede's monograph appeared, another by Albert Schweitzer entitled "The Secret of the Messiahship and the Passion" (also only in German) was also published and this with the exactly opposed view that the "Messiah secret" emanated from Jesus himself. Schweitzer, as we shall see below in Chapter 1, in a later publication (*The Quest of the Historical Jesus*) contrasted his and Wrede's opposing views as representing respectively "thoroughgoing eschatology" (Jesus' own view according to Schweitzer) and "thoroughgoing scepticism" (Wrede's view of the creativity of the church rather than of Jesus).

Thus, at the turn of the century, it must be said that the image of Jesus was broken in two, each half claiming its doughty champion—Wrede or Schweitzer. But this was not to be the end; rather, it was only the beginning of a degree of fragmentation never before experienced in the realm of Biblical studies. And—what is particularly relevant for our present purposes—almost every previously accepted view relative to Jesus Christ (his life's story, his work, his teaching, his claims regarding himself, if any, the nature of his person, his death and resurrection) has been challenged, and in their stead numerous alternative positions have been taken. These it will be the aim of the following chapters to exhibit.

This fragmentation, however, is not without its beneficial results. No longer, for example, may it be said that there is a single view of Jesus that may be labeled "scholarly," any other being equally dubbed "antiquated," or that any one position is, so to speak, in the midstream of scholarly research and all others somewhere on the periphery. Rather, both scholar and lay reader today must face up to the fact that he is being confronted with a number of original and distinctive views of Jesus of Nazareth, all of which may lay claim to be based on adequate scholarship. The problem, the Christian reader finds, is no longer one of knowledge or lack of knowledge of the historical and even archaeological facts involved, nor is it at any rate in most cases a matter of scholarly methodology. The "tools of the trade" and the factual evidence are available to all and for the most part employed by all. The problem today seems, rather, to concern more intangible factors, such as the particular bias or motivation or general predilection of the scholar working over the evidence.

This is not to say, of course, that a given scholar's sincerity is to be challenged; quite the contrary, it is to acknowledge, not alone his sincerity, but also that as an integrated personality his very sincerity is bound to affect his judgments. His sincerity and integration being assumed, his general viewpoints, his active beliefs, the motivating forces of character that "make him tick" cannot but contribute to the conclusions at which he arrives. Because of what the scholar is, he will make certain "assumptions" relative to the importance of certain data in his research as over against other data; he will, in consequence, employ such data rather than others in making up his mind, in de-

ducing his conclusions, and the like. So much is this true
that, with even shallow knowledge of a given scholar's
background and experience, a fair estimate can be made
beforehand as to the results he will attain relative to a
given problem. It is the scholar who denies all this as
applicable in his own case upon whom one has learned to
look with a certain feeling of apprehension.

Again, it should be remarked that the several views
which, as we have said, exhibit some mark of originality
when compared with others present exciting possibilities
relative to the nature, teaching, and work of Jesus Christ.
No one of these views possesses all the truth, and none is
so "far out" but that it has much to contribute to an understanding of him whom the church acknowledges as
"Lord." And whatever else may be said for or against
these images of Jesus of Nazareth, this, at least, is to be
remarked: they leave nothing to be desired in their frank
exposition of the views of the scholars responsible for
them.

A further preliminary observation may be helpful as the
reader glances at the list of images of Jesus noted in the
contents, viz., that the first five chapters deal with what
are essentially "Jewish" views of Jesus and only the last
two with views that may be labeled distinctively "Christian." It was not intended that this should be the case, and
the writer disclaims any intention of having it so. My
meaning is that, though only one of the authors whose
book is examined below is a Jew, yet the first five chapters
deal with writers who endeavor to find a place for Jesus in
the contemporary Jewish ethos, making him out to have
been either an "apocalyptist," a "Rabbi" differing from
other rabbis but on the fringe of the Pharisaic movement,
an "Essene-like figure," a popular type of Messianic claim-
ant, or a "para-Zealot" leader.

This raises a question—one, at any rate, perhaps more. Is there really such a thing as a "Judeo-Christian tradition"? It seems to be assumed on all hands that there is or was such. Is it not nearer the truth of the matter to say rather that the Christian faith broke with Judaism from the start, indeed, that it took its rise *within* Judaism but not *of* it, and that there is sufficient evidence to believe that this break began with Jesus himself? At all events, in this jockeying for position, it is to be noted that only the last two views discussed below make no endeavor to place Jesus anywhere within the compass of orthodox or even of sectarian Judaism. Also it appears equally impressive that with Professor Brandon's recent volume, every niche available within contemporary Judaism has at last been conceded to Jesus. No one, to my knowledge, has suggested that he might have been a Sadducee, but unless it could be demonstrated that he was of the tribe of Levi rather than of Judah, that niche would not have been available to him.

The general reader should note that the problems that are to emerge in the discussion below are for the most part not new to scholarship. Most of them have furnished food for discussion for the past hundred years at least, many of them for much longer than that. All of them are relevant and vital, none trivial. It will perhaps be helpful to list some of the more important. They are as follows:

1. Can one ever hope to discover the mind of Jesus Christ, particularly on the question of his personal identity? that is, in view of the fact that the Gospels were written by the church and that in them we find primarily the image of Jesus as it saw him, can we see through the opacity of the church's Gospels to the real Jesus?

2. Are the terms "Messiah," "Son of Man," "Suffering Servant," "Son of God" always used in the same way by

the various groups contemporary with Jesus (by Jews and pagans, early church, Jesus' immediate disciples, Jesus himself), whether in passages relating to Jesus or another?

3. Did the Christian faith really originate out of any form taken by the Judaism of the first Christian century so that one may think of the two religions as united by any organic bond?

4. If factors appear within the teaching of either Jesus or the early church that one cannot trace to antecedent elements in Judaism, are we then to conclude that these are "pagan" in origin? Is it possible that there is a *tertium quid* (a third source) that in its time had to do battle with both other sources proposed?

5. Are the Gospels and the sources behind them to be adjudged credible? Or must we cast aside as unhistorical and suspect, to say the least, the work of a Christian like Mark, if we must grant that he wrote with an apologetic (that is, a defensive) motive in view?

6. Incidentally, it should be noted that the last question may be applied with equal cogency to the writing of a twentieth-century scholar; if it is admitted, as certainly it must be, that no scholar today writes without a bias relative to every sort of religious problem, does this fact of motive necessarily invalidate the work of the scholar concerned?

7. Again, a question of great importance may be worded thus, Does originality usually lie with the individual or with the community? Specifically, for our present purpose, Did Jesus produce the church or the church, Jesus?

8. Regarding the *Sitz im Leben* (life situation), are we justified in holding that the church simply preserved certain of Jesus' teachings and the narratives relating to him

that the Gospels contain, because it was involved in situations that made such teachings and narratives significant for it? Or, should we go farther and conclude that the church's involvement caused it either to invent certain teachings and narratives and read these back into Jesus' ministry, or at all events to make such changes in the tradition received by it as would fit its case and appear to solve its problems? And, in either case, can we be certain which way we should conclude?

In the end, one imagines the problem of our present concern may be stated in line with either the Socratic maxim so dear to the heart of the modern psychiatrist, "Know thyself," or the Hebrew prophet's characteristic "call" and "mission." Thus, did Jesus of Nazareth "know himself" for what he really was? Did he know what God's will and "call" for him were, what his "mission" in life was? And if so—as for such a superior person as he was, seems a reasonable supposition—have we the means (through the Gospels, by any methodology we may devise) to discover what all these were? For the comfort of the church, if not for its actual continuing existence, it appears vital that we secure an answer to these questions. Can anyone doubt that the church can hardly hope to survive if it is found holding views of the nature of Jesus' person and his work of which he was unaware himself? The present writer does not know of any parallel to such a curious denouement respecting any great personage in any field of human endeavor.

Perhaps the most devastating single factor in the life of the church today is the undoubted fact that by and large the layman does not even know where the theological battle is being waged! The old issues according to popular belief (liberalism versus fundamentalism; science versus religion) if they ever were truly drawn issues, are certainly not so today. This book deals with an issue far beyond and above these older ones, for the religious contest has moved to new sites, and there is no more vital issue under the scrutiny of the Biblical theologian in the present ethos than that of "Which Jesus?"

1

The Apocalyptic "Son of Man"

Of the five interpretations of Jesus of Nazareth that merit the appellative "Jewish," Albert Schweitzer's apocalyptic Jesus was the first to be advanced in the present century. As already remarked, these five interpretations are to be termed Jewish solely for the reason that their authors consider one or other of the Jewish categories adequate for cataloging Jesus. *Apocalypticism* originated within the Jewish culture about 175 B.C., secured much popular approval during Judaism's period of despondency in the late Greek and early Roman eras, came into disfavor with the rabbis between the Jewish Wars of A.D. 66 and 135, and remained acceptable only within Christian circles in the late first and second centuries. Broadly speaking, Schweitzer interpreted Jesus as one standing in this apocalyptic stream because he believed Jesus used the term "Son of Man" of himself after the fashion of Dan. 7:13, or at any rate as this figure coming "with the clouds of heaven" might be represented by an individual chosen to act as God's mediator in his coming reign.

Schweitzer presents his view of the Jesus who as "Son of Man" conceived himself about to return shortly and set up God's Kingdom on earth, in the last chapter of his epochal volume entitled *The Quest of the Historical Jesus*. In the

first part of that chapter, he delineates his own view which
he terms "thoroughgoing eschatology" with the use of Wilhelm Wrede's "thoroughgoing scepticism" as a buffer, indicating point for point how opposed the one view is to the
other. This device proves both ingenious and informative.

Schweitzer was able to use Wrede's opposing thesis in
this way because, as indicated in the Introduction, above,
on the same day they had previously published mono-
graphs that agreed in two items. These were: (a) that
Mark's Gospel is constructed of a vast number of discon-
nected passages (pericopes), the ligatures between which
are not to be thought original as they lay in the tradition
but were added by either Mark or another in order to
bring meaning and unity to the whole (SQ-336); and (b)
that a "dogmatic element"—the "Messiah secret"—is su-
perimposed on Mark's Gospel (SQ-336) in such a way as
to control the actual historical narrative throughout. That
is to say, everything that happens in the narrative happens
because of the secret which, accordingly, must either be
contemporary with Jesus and reflect his mind or else have
nothing to do with him and the actual turn of events, being
in this case a fabrication of the church "out of whole
cloth." Of these alternatives, Schweitzer subscribed to the
first, Wrede to the second.

Wrede held in fact that Jesus never conceived of himself
in Messianic terms; such an idea first arose in the later
church, and as a result of its discomfiture, it invented the
conception of a "Messiah secret" which Jesus was incor-
rectly said to have originated and to have ordered kept
until after his resurrection. Such is, Schweitzer declares,
Wrede's "thoroughgoing scepticism" (cf. App. 1).

Schweitzer, contrariwise, takes the other tack, accepting
Jesus as the originator of the "Messiah secret" and so of
the dogmatic element controlling the Gospel narrative

(SQ-338). His argument is directed toward the development of the thesis that it was Jesus' emphasis upon his living in the "last times" (the *eschaton,* to use the Greek term for this period) that motivated all Jesus' teaching and activity—nothing, indeed, that he ever did or taught lacked this eschatological element and awareness. Hence, Schweitzer named his interpretation "thoroughgoing eschatology," meaning thereby to characterize, not his own view of Jesus and his message merely as the opposing phrase reflects Wrede's judgment of Jesus, but rather Jesus' views of himself as "Son of Man" and the Kingdom as shortly to be brought into historical actuality. As for the possibility of a third, mediating, view lying somewhere between or about the other two, Schweitzer declares, *"Tertium non datur"* (SQ-337)!

In the end, it is to be remarked, Schweitzer believed Jesus' apocalypticism to be so "far out" (that is, so far removed from what modern man can accept) that he had no hope of making Jesus relevant in our day or of securing acceptance for his extremely fanciful teachings (SQ-398 f.). In consequence, on purely pragmatic grounds, at any rate, one wonders why Schweitzer should have been so concerned to oppose Wrede's views. No doubt from the purely scholarly interest, it is a matter of concern whether it was Jesus or the church that entertained the eschatological views found in Mark's Gospel. But if neither alternative is ultimately important to the church and its presentation of the gospel, the dispute becomes very much a "fighting with windmills," and it will be a sad day for the Kingdom if there is, as Schweitzer claims, no "third way" in the matter. It is part of our aim in writing this book to show that the scholarship of the past sixty years has dismissed this dilemma as unreal and has come up with a *tertium,* indeed also a *quartum,* a *quintum,* etc.

Meanwhile, however, Schweitzer's attack on the "Old Liberalism's" interpretation of Jesus as a mere preacher of an ethical Kingdom of God on earth, a glorified but always human rabbi, an all-too-modern apologete for the particular brand of idealism held by the liberal interpreter, makes salutary reading. That such a "Jesus," as Schweitzer was keen to show, "never had any existence" (SQ-398), must give us pause lest the necromancers of a ghost that this genius claims to have forever laid to rest should again endeavor to call it back to life.

As for Schweitzer's view that the apocalyptic outlook dominated Jesus' entire teaching and activities, he argues as follows:

First, *the entire series of events recorded in Mark's Gospel which culminates in Jesus' choice and sending forth of his disciples* was presented with a view "to set in motion the eschatological development of history" (SQ-371). That is to say, from Jesus' reading of the apocalyptic literature of his people, he came to believe that it was encumbent on the Son of Man to engage actively in a series of dynamic events that would set history in motion and bring about God's ultimate purpose as understood by the apocalyptists. At this early stage in his ministry, Jesus, according to Schweitzer, expected the Kingdom of God (interpreted always in the eschatological sense, that is, as God's Reign to be achieved only at the end of history) would come "at harvest time" (SQ-358; see Matt. 10:23 and App. 2). However, this "prediction was not fulfilled" (SQ-359); the course of events or "actual history" did not follow the "dogmatic history"—neither the "woes of the Messiah," the gift of the Spirit, nor the "Parousia of the Son of Man" occurred (SQ-364). Schweitzer calls this "the first postponement of the Parousia" (SQ-360).

Secondly, Jesus believed that Elijah (Schweitzer's spelling is "Elias") must come before the appearance of the Son of Man (Mal. 4:5). Accordingly, that Jesus might "somehow drag or force the eschatological events into the framework" of his ministry and its attendant circumstances, he called John the Baptist Elijah, solely with a view to the prophesied sequence of events occurring (SQ-376).

Thirdly, like the baptism practiced by John the Baptist which Schweitzer conceived as an eschatological sacrament (SQ-378), Jesus' feeding of the five thousand, the baptism of the Spirit, and the Last Supper of Passion Week also fit into this category (SQ-378-380). For Jesus, these were all examples of "the Messianic feast" and as such indirectly showed him disclosing "the Messianic secret" to his disciples (SQ-382). Such events indicate Jesus as throughout motivated by "the dogmatic element in the history" (SQ-381).

Fourthly, it is because of these "psychological conditions" shared by Jesus and his disciples with the contemporary apocalyptic writers that he with Peter, James, and John had the vision that declared Jesus to be the Messiah (SQ-386). This, of course, was the experience of the transfiguration which Schweitzer held to have preceded Peter's confession at Caesarea Philippi. This reversal of the ordering of the two events made it intelligible, Schweitzer held, that Jesus should say to Peter, "Flesh and blood has not revealed this to you, but my Father who is in heaven" (Matt. 16:17).

Fifthly, Jesus' predictions of his own sufferings and death "that the Kingdom might come" (SQ-389), which Schweitzer held are correctly attributed to him, were the result of his conviction arrived at through further study of

the Scriptures following the "first postponement" referred
to above. At first, Jesus had attached the concept of
suffering (*peirosmos*) only to his disciples, but when at
the sending forth of the Twelve, the Kingdom did not
come (Matt. 10:23), Jesus dissociated the sufferings from
his disciples and came to believe that they were to apply
to himself alone as the Messianic Son of Man (SQ-389).
As a consequence, preceding Passion Week, "Jesus sets
out for Jerusalem, solely in order to die there" (SQ-391),
and so finally to force the Kingdom to come (SQ-389),
391)!

Sixthly, it is clear, Schweitzer contends, that the significant events of Passion Week are all under the authority of
Jesus who is in complete control of the situation; everything, indeed, during this week occurs when and where he
determines shall be the case. These events include: the
so-called triumphal entry (SQ-393), the "invective against
the Pharisees" (SQ-395), the question about David's son
and David's Lord (SQ-395), Judas' betrayal of Jesus'
Messiah-consciousness to the high priest and Jesus' consequent admission of the same at his trial (SQ-396 f.),
and the revealing of it to the people by the high priest and
his associates in the courtyard of Pilate (SQ-397). All
these events, set in motion by Jesus, constitute in Schweitzer's view the final proof that he conceived of himself in
terms of the Messianic Son of Man who would at once
usher in the Kingdom of God through his death and triumphant resurrection, so bringing an end to history. As for
the difficult saying at Mark 14:28, Schweitzer interpreted
this to mean that Jesus contemplated returning with his
disciples, "at their head," so to speak, "from Jerusalem to
Galilee," there to set up the Kingdom. This remained,
however, an "unfulfilled saying" (SQ-388).

CRITIQUE

Biblical scholarship has come a long way since Schweitzer first wrote his *Quest* (in German in 1906), and the archaeologist and historian have both had much to say of value in the interim. Accordingly, much of the minutiae with which he deals will have to come before us in the context of later thought, and it is scarcely worth our while to examine it in detail. We shall content ourselves here, therefore, with several observations of a general nature that will be found to carry over for value to our consideration of the work of others studied, looking at but two or three of the details of Schweitzer's argument.

First, then, it is to be noted that Schweitzer's argument is based on what C. C. McCown calls the "either-or fallacy," the "fallacy of antithesis," and the like, and as McCown further observes, Schweitzer's "own theory may be demolished by the same specious, illogical arguments by which he disproves others" (see MSRJ-252). The proof of McCown's contention can easily be demonstrated from the long history of German Biblical and theological scholarship, and particularly from Schweitzer's own writing. For, he saw the three great landmarks of progress in the realm of New Testament theology to consist in the laying down of three alternatives and the selection in each case of the right one: by David Friedrich Strauss in the early nineteenth century of the alternative "*either* purely historical *or* purely supernatural"; by the Tübingen school at about the same period of another alternative, "*either* Synoptic *or* Johannine"; and by Johannes Weiss near the close of the century of still another, "*either* eschatological

or non-eschatological." Schweitzer held that "progress always consists in taking one or other of (these) two alternatives, in abandoning the attempt to combine them." Accordingly, he joined forces with Weiss in this last choice,
holding that the Kingdom of God for Jesus lay only and
wholly in the future, where also the exercise of his own
Messiahship (his coming as the Son of Man—"a purely
eschatological designation of the Messiah") would be
found, as well as with Weiss's view that the ethic of Jesus
was merely a "penitential discipline" (what Schweitzer
termed an *Interimsethik*) to fit men in this life for entering
the apocalyptic Kingdom.

For this writer, and for most British and American
scholars working in the Biblical field, the posing of the
"either-or" dialectic smacks of the philosophic type of
theologian rather than of the scientific Biblical scholar.
For, the latter accords with the scientific method adopted
in other fields of research in attempting to construct the
edifice of learning on the work of his predecessors, adding
here a little and there a little, quite content if his labors
shall eventuate in the addition of a single brick or stone in
the fabric of the house of truth. Theologians, and particularly Teutonic theologians, appear rather to think that
they may "begin at scratch" in constructing their
"systems." This method—arrogant though it seems—has
intrigued the German Biblical scholar as well, no doubt
because the German classicist has traditionally studied the
philosophers rather than the scientists. The lay reader will
do well to ask himself whether a student of the Biblical
data which is so largely of a historical nature ought not
ally himself rather more closely with the scientist and his
techniques of research than with the philosopher and his
cerebrally originated systems. The scientist characteristi-
cally goes on "looking for honey wherever it may be

found," and at times this is in the most unlikely places, often enough in the very "tents of his enemies"!

Secondly, as we have already hinted, Schweitzer's own following out of the "either-or" dialectic in opposition to Wrede's views has resulted merely in his tying down the historic Jesus to another camp within the contemporary Judaism as against that elected by his opponent. This raises a problem that will be found to carry through much of our discussion in this book, viz., if after all our research, we can arrive at no higher estimate of Jesus of Nazareth than that he was circumscribed by the necessity of making a choice between parties in the current Judaism, does it matter very much which party we find him to have allied himself with? Or, to state the problem in a slightly different manner, in one, indeed, that may open up new vistas, is it so certain that the historic Jesus had no other avenue(s) open to him than the contemporary Jewish views? Is this not in a priori fashion to deny him the quality of originality? By what right do we do this? Is it possible, indeed, that it is the twentieth-century scholar, and not the first-century Jesus, who in his thinking is circumscribed by the limitations of the Judaism of that day as he makes his research?

At all events, it is noteworthy that the issue of Schweitzer's work is this: in Schweitzer we have the anomaly of a scholar who does not belong to his own school of thought! Not, that is to say, so far as to be prepared to identify himself with this apocalyptic Jesus (his thought and teaching) who emerges from Schweitzer's painstaking labors. For, in the end both Wrede and Schweitzer lead us to a Jesus who is for our times "a stranger and an enigma" (SQ-399). Both give us a Christ who has fundamentally no message for our day, no teaching from which we may learn anything leading to the good life for ourselves or

others. Little wonder that Schweitzer himself found more
of value in following Jesus' actions than his words, as the
Master mistakenly (according to the disciple) assayed the
role of the apocalyptic "Son of Man" believing this to be
the Father's will for him, while the disciple (accepting the
same will for himself) gave up his Biblical chair in a famous university, studied medicine, and went out to Africa
to care for the poor and needy.

Thirdly, Schweitzer's use of the Gospel data even for
his own day was partly obscurantist, partly illustrative of
the untenable attempt to dichotomize it, accepting only the
part that appealed to his (a particular scholar's) theological approach to the Biblical materials. Indeed, these two
characteristics often joined forces in Biblical scholarship,
as may be abundantly illustrated from the writings of the
day. In Schweitzer's case, a remarkable example of both
tendencies may be seen in his interpretation of Matt.
10:23. A short discussion of the passage will be found in
Appendix 2. To what is said there we would only add that
an examination of the verse shows it to be in immediate
contact both before and after with verses spoken certainly
at a later date. It cannot be argued, therefore, as Schweitzer does, that at a very early date in his ministry, Jesus expected the Parousia and the coming of the Kingdom as im-
minent, and that such prediction on his part "was not
fulfilled" (SQ-359). On the contrary, it may be maintained
that the saying belongs to a context wherein Jesus was
speaking of the founding of his fellowship, his disciples
being a nucleus for the same and instruments looking
toward its growth, and so in this sense of the Kingdom's
coming.

The same analysis of the data does away with the idea
of early prediction of "persecution" (*peirosmos*) and hatred of the disciples at a time in the ministry when nothing

suggested such attitudes on the part of Jesus' enemies. Schweitzer brings in some of the verses contiguous to v. 23 in Matt., ch. 10, to which reference was made in the preceding paragraph (vs. 17-22, 24-33; SQ-387-389), in order to demonstrate the existence or at least possibility of such an attitude. But these verses belong to the eschatological discourse of Passion Week (if they be ascribed to Jesus at all!). One of Schweitzer's main supports for his thesis, therefore, to the effect that Jesus would force the eschatological events to come to pass (for example, the "persecution" as of necessity preceding the Messianic reign), including the idea that he "sets out for Jerusalem, solely in order to die there" (SQ-391), and solely with a view to forcing "dogmatic history" upon real history, is seen to be untenable. For, it is based on a *dating* of the teachings of Jesus and a forced exegesis of the same that is unwarranted.

The same sort of forced interpretation is characteristic throughout Schweitzer's elaboration of his views. The writer has personally counted 115 points wherein his exegesis, definitions, or conclusions reflect a bias about which there may be said to be at least a reasonable doubt that the end product reflects the mind of the historic Jesus with whom he is dealing. No doubt others would make up an even longer list!

Finally, it is to be noted that Schweitzer's "thoroughgoing eschatology" as a vehicle for representing the mind of Jesus of Nazareth, while such a title suggests a point of view rather widely acceptable to many modern Biblical scholars, yet is open to considerable question. The point of view is this—that in the development of Hebrew-Jewish thought and theology, the apocalyptist chronologically and, to an extent at least, logically followed the prophet. It is pointed out that the apocalyptic literature was devel-

oped in a time of gloom and despair while the Jews were
suffering under Hellenistic rule (2d century B.C.), and
that the divine message that came to them was, accordingly, one of comfort and of a hope based upon belief in a
future life in which God would give solace to his people.

Whether this explains the sequence of the Hebrew prophetic and apocalyptic literatures and the marked differences of teaching and spirit that existed between them or
not, the problem of Jesus' allegiance to the one or other
remains. Even if it be granted that elements of both types
of literature are to be found in his teaching, the degree to
which he may be thought to have attached himself to
apocalyptic modes of thought and expression still remains
in question. Was this, for example, sufficient to justify
speaking of his views as "thoroughgoing eschatology"? Was
it, indeed, characterized by the fantastic sort of expression
that results necessarily in the "modern man" finding it necessary to discard Jesus' teaching as utterly unacceptable
and incapable of teaching him anything of worth, as
Schweitzer acknowledges to be the case?

Bultmann, for one, while agreeing that Jesus by and
large did accept the "apocalyptic picture of the future,"
contends that he did so "with significant reduction of detail," and he thinks that, though for Jesus there were naturally "signs of the time," these were not of the sort for
which "apocalyptic fantasy peers" (BNTTh-6). Bornkamm, too, while allowing that without the background of
Jewish apocalyptic, "the message of Jesus . . . can never
be understood" (BJN-39), yet refuses to categorize Jesus
with the "apocalyptic visionaries" of his day; above all, he
will not allow that Jesus appealed to "ecstatic states of
mind and visions," to "secret revelations of the next world,"
or to "miraculous insight into God's decrees," as the
apocalyptist did with a view to validating his teachings and

message (BJN-56). The present writer has given considerable thought to a comparison of the Synoptic teaching with Jewish apocalypticism (BRM-Ch. 12), and he would agree with Maurice Goguel (*The Life of Jesus,* 1933; pp. 312 f.) and with W. G. Kümmel (KPF-103 f.), that, while Jesus in the generic sense of the term had an eschatological message (that is, he believed that God's Reign had finally come in and through himself, his teaching and his work), yet his thought was "in complete contrast to the 'Weltanschauung' of apocalyptic," the world view which, if we understand Schweitzer aright, was just exactly that of the "thoroughgoing eschatology" which he would attribute to Jesus.

2

The Existentialist Rabbi

Rudolf Bultmann was Wilhelm Wrede's most brilliant proselyte, and he followed that acme of "Old Liberal" skepticism in basically conceiving of Jesus as a somewhat heretical rabbi. But numerous other forces as well impinged on the creative mind of the Marburg giant, so that one has come almost to think of him as belonging to a category in the realm of Biblical studies that is severely his own. To understand him, then, it is essential that the student look carefully at the several great influences that have affected Bultmann's intellectual life.

Fortunately, these are not hard to discover, and, indeed, for two reasons Bultmann is the most readily described Biblical theologian of the present century. In a sense these reasons are one. In the first place, he has excelled every other N.T. scholar among his contemporaries and for perhaps the past hundred years in stimulating discussion on the themes with which he deals. Needless to say, in this scholarly dialogue Bultmann's own ideas have been the focus of everything that has been said and written and his views of Jesus have, accordingly, become an open book among Christian thinkers everywhere. Secondly, and in consequence of the heated debate that has ensued, Bultmann has been forced to indulge in much self-analysis and repartee, and particularly to lay bare the germinal centers in which his ideas have originated. And, as a result it may be said that Bultmann is the outstanding example of much theological scholarship that has taken to itself the techniques or expertise and findings in many fields of human inquiry that ushered in the twentieth century. Add to this, however, that Bultmann has himself invented or at least aided in shaping and sharpening many of the tools required in these trades.

Briefly, these various influences which have shaped Bultmann's views are first, as already remarked, the thought of Wilhelm Wrede, and this in two directions:

a. One was in the matter of the Marcan ligatures (local, temporal, logical) of which we have said that both Schweitzer and Wrede independently asserted they had not come to Mark in the primitive tradition Bultmann was following. That is to say, the separate passages, whether in the teaching or narrative portions, had been so used by the evangelists and teachers that preceded Mark as they witnessed to the Gospel that Mark, then, had pieced these sections together, employing the ligatures mentioned (obviously, his own) to make a continuous account of the teaching and ministry of Jesus. It would seem obvious, too —or so it has seemed to Wrede, Bultmann, and their successors—that Mark in piecing together these elements of the tradition did so in a way to reflect his own bias relative to Jesus' significance and supposed claims.

In at least two passages, Bultmann writes of his debt to Wrede at this point. One of these is in *The History of the Synoptic Tradition* (BHST-1), where he writes of Mark as having "arranged the traditional material . . . in the light of the faith of the early Church." The other is in the opening section of his *The Theology of the New Testament* (BNTTh-3), where, though he does not refer specifically to Wrede, yet as in the *History* on the basis of Wrede's work, he distinguishes in the Synoptics the "old tradition," "ideas" of the church itself, and the "editorial work" of Mark and the others. In both of these works, then, as also in his *Jesus and the Word* and elsewhere in his writings, Bultmann has employed this analysis with relentless zeal and powerful results. His dissection of the Gospel materials in these works is the net product, one might almost say the necessary result, of his following through of Wrede's thesis to its utmost logical conclusion. Space does not permit of a proper evaluation of Bultmann's conclusions here, but in Appendix 3 will be found a short résumé of the findings of form criticism for the reader who is unacquainted with this phenomenon.

b. Bultmann is equally candid in ascribing to Wrede's skepticism his own acceptance of the "Messiah secret" theory. According to Mark, Jesus in his word and work spoke and acted as the Messiah, but he cautioned his disciples and the demons not to make him known (in the former case, not till after the resurrection). This "secret" according to Wrede and Bultmann did not represent the mind of Jesus in the matter, though as we have seen it did so according to Schweitzer. Rather, the two former held it was the church that believed in Jesus as the Messiah and so concocted the idea of the secret and then read it back into Jesus' mind, so to speak, to cover its own embarrassment in finding no evidence in the tradition that Jesus so thought of himself! (BNTTh-32 and 26 f.; see also App. 1, below.) Bultmann deals rather harshly with any who attempt to find historic validity in the suggestion that the secret originated with Jesus; for, says he, the secret is to be found only in the "editorial sentences" (i.e., in the Marcan ligatures mentioned above) and not in the body of the pericopes, or passages, that had come down in the tradition to Mark. To believe that the secret had originated with Jesus would also require us to believe that Jesus had "spiritualized" the Messiah concept before applying it to himself, and of this Bultmann claims there is no evidence.

The second major influence which Bultmann acknowledges as formative in his thinking is the study of the Teutonic, Greco-Roman, Hindu and Buddhistic, as well as other mythologies. This study has provided Bultmann with several of the categories which he employs in analyzing the history of the Gospel tradition, such as legends, myths, apothegms, and has furnished him with much information relative to the formation of tradition in general. Particularly it may be said that Bultmann's mythological studies have lent themselves as an aid to a reinterpretation of certain elements of the Biblical tradition taken over from the Hebrew prophets and apocalyptists.

In making this reinterpretation he finds it possible, for example, as a result of these studies, to speak of the "mythological eschatology" that permeates such writings (BJCM-Ch. II), and he writes without hesitancy that "New Testament scholars are at variance as to whether Jesus himself claimed to be the Messiah, the King of the time of blessedness, whether he believed himself to be the Son of Man who would come on the clouds of heaven. If so, Jesus understood himself in the light of mythology. We need not, at this point, decide one way or the other. At any rate, the early Christian community thus regarded him as a mythological figure." Similarly, in discussing the completed Gospels, Bultmann writes, "The mythical element is stronger in Mark than in either Matthew or Luke." This, he says, is true, in spite of the fact that Matthew and Luke add mythical items such as the infancy narratives which Mark does not have, because regarding the two later Gospels the observation holds that "in the whole outline the Christ myth recedes in favour of the picture of the earthly ministry of Jesus" (BHST-348).

Obviously, this mythological reinterpretation of the Biblical data, including particularly an understanding of such terms as "Christ" ("Messiah"), "Son of Man," "Kingdom of God," and the rest that the Gospels have taken over from the prophetic and apocalyptic literatures, fits in very neatly with Bultmann's acceptance of Wrede's two points mentioned above (his views on the trustworthiness of the Marcan connectives and his skepticism relative to a Messianic consciousness on Jesus' part). It takes time for such an elaborate mythology, such as Bultmann finds in the Bible—with its three-storied universe, its population of angels, demonic powers, gods and goddesses, and the like—to develop, and when it does, moreover, it does so in terms of the world of thought of the contemporary peoples of the age. Generally speaking, then, the Gospels' mythology as it stands is more likely to represent the mind of the later church than that of Jesus of Nazareth, though no judgment is for the moment required of us on this point.

Suffice it to say, that for Bultmann, such mythology "is different from the conception of the world which has been formed and developed by science since its inception in ancient Greece and which has been accepted by all modern men" (BJCM-15). And since this is so, Bultmann holds that for an understanding of the gospel, modern man requires to have all these Biblical data "demythologized."

Finally, Bultmann frankly acknowledges his debt to existentialism and particularly to that of Martin Heidegger for its contribution of both a method and a new mythology to displace that of the Bible, by means of which one may present the one gospel in a manner acceptable to modern man. Existentialism derives its name and definition from its view of human "personality" as, not a "substance" lying behind or underneath, but rather as an "I" that is "ever-growing, ever-becoming, ever-increasing." And this "I" that is ever seeking "to be realized" achieves its existence through making decisions that it is called upon to make as it is, so to speak, "put on the spot" and challenged. Thus, a "human being," as it were, "chooses its genuine existence by resolution."

For the historian, this thought of Heidegger justifies the writing of "autobiography" for the reason that "personality experiences its own history within the frame of universal history and interwoven within it" (see Bultmann's *The Presence of Eternity*, BPE-146). For the Biblical scholar, it calls for a reevaluation of the Bible's *mythological* eschatology. This is a pressing need today because "the kerygma is incredible to modern man, for he is convinced that the mythical view of the world is obsolete" (see Bultmann's essay in *Kerygma and Myth,* BKM-3). Rather than throw away the gospel, says Bultmann, what is required today, therefore, is to discard the *obsolete* wrapping in which it comes to us in the New Testament and substitute an *existential* wrapping whereby the modern man can be confronted in a realistic way with the kerygma. In such confrontation the person comes face to face with what becomes for him his own private eschatology, and in this moment of "resolution" it may honestly be said of him that "his future is now." In thus making the substitution of an *existential* eschatology which modern man can understand and appreciate for one that first-century man could accept, Bultmann contends we have succeeded in preserving the timeless element in the gospel so that nothing is lost.

STATEMENT OF BULTMANN'S ANALYSIS
OF JESUS' THOUGHT AND MINISTRY

It is rather amazing to discover how little Bultmann's thought about Jesus and his message developed from 1926, when his *Jesus* was first published in German, to 1951 with the translation of his *The Theology of the New Testament,* Vol. I, into English. Even the outline of Jesus' teaching as presented in the two books is throughout essentially the same, following the pattern which we shall adopt below. As for Bultmann's debt to Wrede in the matter of the "Messiah secret" and Messianic consciousness, the point is clearly presented in a long and involved section in the *Theology* (BNTTh-26-32), in which Bultmann devotes seven of his thirty pages comprising the chapter on "The Message of Jesus" to an elaboration of his views on this subject. In the English translation of the former book (entitled *Jesus and the Word*, 1934), a like section does not occur, but Bultmann deals with the issue, taking the same position as in the *Theology,* in the chapter entitled "View-point and Method" and at other passages in the body of the book (see BNTTh-28 f., 38 f., 64, and 123-126 particularly).

As an understanding of Bultmann's views relative to Jesus' awareness about himself and his mission is so fundamental to the whole, we shall begin our analysis of "The Message of Jesus" as Bultmann sees it.

1. *The Question of Jesus' Self-awareness*

On this point, Bultmann writes quite clearly, "It was not as a king, but as a prophet and a rabbi that Jesus appeared"; he is also prepared to employ the Talmud's ap-

pellative for Jesus, viz., "an exorcist" (BNTTh-27). This
is as far as Bultmann ever goes anywhere in his writings,
so far as this writer has been able to discover, and it should
be added that his use of the term "prophet" is quite limited;
as far as can be seen, it is only in the context of the next
subject to be discussed, that of the coming of the Kingdom
in an existential sense, that our author uses this title.

It is quite true, Bultmann proceeds to remark, that the
early church, in one or other of its stages of development,
declared its belief in Jesus as the Danielic "Son of Man,"
or the Deutero-Isaianic "Suffering Servant," and the like.
But, he believes, these suggestions as to what might be
termed a "high Christology" never emanate from Jesus'
words, as found in the oldest strata of the tradition. Nor
was Jesus' career, when "measured by traditional messianic ideas," *"messianic"* (BNTTh-27). Nor again is there
any evidence that Jesus reinterpreted the *"Messiah-
concept"* as this has been traditionally held by the Jews,
so that one might speak of him as a spiritual Messiah
rather than as a political one (BNTTh-28). Nor, finally,
does Jesus ever speak of himself in terms of a "futuristic"
Messiahship (BNTTh-29).

In his discussion of all views that conceive of Jesus'
self-awareness along such lines as we have just mentioned,
Bultmann returns to his careful analysis of the Synoptic
tradition and finds such views wanting of verification.
Where, he asks for example, in what may be adjudged au-
thentic teachings of Jesus, can any "polemic" be found
that is oriented "against the conventional Messiah-
concept" (BNTTh-28)? Again, as for a view like
Schweitzer's that Jesus would return after his death and
resurrection as the Son of Man on the clouds of heaven,
an analysis of the sources in the oral tradition shows that
we are here dealing with two sets of tradition. The first

(that referring to death and resurrection) is late tradition and may be categorized as *vacticinium ex eventu* (i.e., prophecy after the happening), it never appears in the source Q (BNTTh-29, 30). Also, although Q does report sayings about the Parousia, these always refer to the Son of Man "in the third person" and have in consequence no reference to Jesus himself (BNTTh-30).

The upshot of Bultmann's work is his conclusion, flatly and without hesitancy stated, that wherever "the passion" of Jesus is in question, the "Messiah-Son-of-Man" concept is "singularly enriched" with the thought of "suffering, dying, rising"—a combination of ideas quite "unknown to Judaism." But, such enrichment was contributed "not by Jesus himself but by the Church *ex eventu*" (BNTTh-31). Herein, as already stated, Bultmann follows in the footsteps of Wrede as he analyzes out the "dogmatic element" that overlies the "real history" in the Gospels.

2. The Question of Jesus' Message

Jesus' teaching as prophetic rabbi involves a rather simple, direct, but withal challenging appeal to his people of the Jews with whom he wholly identifies himself and beyond whom (as Harnack had also declared) he never looks in the direction of a Gentile mission (BJW-43). Essentially, Jesus' message, then, does not carry us beyond the following three points:

a. *"The Eschatological Message."* Jesus stood within the context of the apocalypticism of his times, as Schweitzer had already seen, and in general he accepted the concepts involved. These included the ideas that this age or aeon was wholly given over to Satan and his forces, that God's Reign would take over and destroy these, so ushering in a godly aeon, that this would bring salvation to

God's people, and that in its entirety this change would prove "a miraculous event" whose author would be God alone, no man's help being sought or required to accomplish it (BNTTh-4 f.). Jesus took over this picture from the apocalyptists, but "with significant reduction of detail" (BNTTh-6).

The element in the whole picture as presented by Jesus that is distinctive of himself and "really his own" lies in the assurance with which he declares: *"Now the time is come! God's Reign is breaking in! The end is here!"* (BNTTh-6). As for "signs of the time" by which men may know that it has arrived, these are not at all of the type that the apocalyptists' fancy had conjured up (cosmic events and the like in the external world); rather they are "himself" alone (that is, *"His presence, his deeds, his message!"* (BNTTh-7). By this, Jesus meant, not that the Kingdom of God had already come, but that it was "dawning," that it was "now breaking in" (BNTTh-9).

Obviously, therefore (and *here Bultmann's existentialism stands him in good stead*), every man must "get ready" or else "keep ready" for its appearance. For, "now is the *time of decision*" (BNTTh-9), and all men are now confronted with "deciding" on a choice between "God," on the one hand, "worldly goods" or values, on the other (BNTTh-10). This is not asceticism, to be sure, for it has as its ultimate goal the positive value suggested at all times by such phrases as "fulfilment of God's will," "readiness for God's demand" on one's life (BNTTh-11).

b. *"The Demand of God."* In his two books with which we are dealing, Bultmann devotes twice as much space to the matter of the demand or will of God as to the problem of eschatology. This is because he finds it important to contrast Jesus' attitude toward the moral problem with "Jewish legalism" (BNTTh-11). The Jewish attitude toward God's will as expressed in the Mosaic law makes no real distinction between the references of the laws involved—whether they be ritual, moral, religious, cultic, or other. All are alike to be obeyed *as laws,* not because of any value attaching to such obedience as measured by the end product, but rather because all alike have been declared by God himself. It is the *source* and not the motivation of a given command that makes it important or otherwise.

This attitude is to Jesus' mind pious nonsense. What God requires of man is, not such rote compliance, but "radical obedience," and "radical obedience is only possible where a man understands the demand and affirms it from within himself" (BNTTh-12). And this means that man's inner attitudes, his secret motivations, his desires and purposes, are more important than any outward expression in word or deed that they may assume or to which they may give rise. "Anger," "name-calling," "evil desire," "insincerity"—such are God's concern, and not principally "overt acts of murder, adultery, and perjury," or any similar actions with which the courts can deal (BNTTh-13).

Thus, Jesus as "prophetic rabbi," though he does not specifically declare against the O.T. law for its own day and ethos, does pick and choose among its demands as applicable for his contemporary scene and suggests reasons for a law's applicability in one context or for one reason and not in another context or for another reason (BNTTh-15). The laws relative to divorce and tithing are cases in point (Mark 10:2-9; Matt. 23:23 f.). In all such cases, Jesus assumes an attitude toward the O.T. that no rabbi would ever have thought of doing, viz., he "critically distinguishes the important from the unimportant, the essential from the indifferent" (BNTTh-16).

The "radical obedience," then, which Jesus demands is essentially "the demand for love"—this alone is what God really wants, and aside from love there is no genuine obedience (BNTTh-18 ff.). And here it becomes clear in what sense Jesus' "eschatological" and "ethical" teachings really "constitute a unity." This unity is not achieved, as some think, through the formation of either "ethical character" or "ethical social order." It is achieved, rather, "in the concrete moment" of decision, as "the eschatological proclamation" of God's coming Reign and the "ethical demand" which it will entail are brought home to each man's consciousness, so that he stands before God and "God stands before him." Both of these (proclamation and demand) "direct him into his Now as the decision for God" (BNTTh-21). Here again, as is obvious, Bultmann's existentialism stands him in good stead.

c. *"Jesus' Idea of God."* And again, in his interpretation of Jesus' idea of God, *Bultmann's existentialism has a major part to play.* For, though it is true that Jesus expected God's Reign in the final sense of the end of all things and the "making of all things new" and in this was disappointed, yet it is not in this belief of the nearness of the end that what is essential to the "eschatological message" really lies. The Hebrew prophets also thought and spoke of the near coming of God's judgment; this was because they were so overwhelmingly aware of God and of his will for man that this world with its small claims seemed to fade from the picture (BNTTh-22 f.).

So it was with Jesus. It is his thought of God and of man's dependence on him that matters in all he says of the nearness of the Reign of God.

What was that thought of God that Jesus entertained? Up to a point it was identical with that of other rabbis of his day. God was Creator, Sustainer, Governor of the world. But, whereas with the coming of apocalyptic, God had retreated to such a distance as almost to become irrelevant (one to whom high-sounding prayer must be offered thrice a day), for Jesus he became near as "Father." Law and *Mishnah* (tradition) had also come between God and the average rabbi. But for Jesus, God becomes the "Demander" for every man that his will be obeyed in the existential moment of decision (BNTTh-24).

This same individualization of God's relationship with man appears in the absence of all reference to the history of the Nation in Jesus' speaking about God. For him, God was interested, not so much in the Jews as a people, as in this Jew and that Jew as an individual, as a person. It is, then, "in his own little history" that God meets with a man, with a "de-historized man," that is, with a man whose ties are all severed from his nation's history and so from the "security" that attaches to such a group connection (BNTTh-25 f.).

For Bultmann, as we have said, Jesus' teaching is simple and direct, but eminently challenging. It is also extremely unified; the eschatological proclamation of God's Reign brings with it God's demand upon every man's life, and in both it is the presence of God who stands before every man and confronts him as an individual that is all-important. It is God who challenges and demands of each man that his will be done, and in that confrontation, for each man God's Reign is about to begin.

CRITIQUE OF BULTMANN'S IMAGE OF JESUS

To write a criticism of Bultmann's work is as difficult as to lay bare the sources of his thought is easy. All who have been at work in the N.T. field for the past half century owe much to his powers of insight, his fastidious, discriminating ability, his clarity of expression, his persuasiveness. All these elements that go to characterize the scholar and his efforts are so obviously appealing and influential that to evaluate his work is to evaluate that of most of his contemporaries, for almost all would willingly acknowledge their debt to him.

And yet, to uncover the existentialist Rabbi hidden beneath the debris of myth and legend which according to Bultmann the early church had unloaded on him was not so difficult a task, given the fine assortment of tools Bultmann was able to assemble. Wrede's work on Mark's connectives and his "Messiah secret," Heidegger's existentialist philosophy, and the work of the school of Comparative Religions (*Religionsgeschichte*) on the various ethnic mythologies—such composed Bultmann's tool kit. Even the makings of the Rabbi were present in the estimate of Jesus that Harnack and his colleagues of the "Old Liberal" school left behind them for Bultmann to take up and reshape. Thus, both tools and rough casting of the image of Jesus of Nazareth came readily to hand that Bultmann's acute mind might deal with them to new ends. This he did with superb effectiveness.

In spite of this effectiveness, however, and the large following Bultmann has achieved, one must express grave doubts that the emasculated image of Jesus Christ which he presents to the world will long endure. Indeed, there have been signs for some years that Bultmann's work lacks lasting appeal. Witness the so-called "post-Bultmannian school" whose slogan might be phrased— "Through the wilderness of Bultmann to the promised land beyond." Such a slogan if such there be, let us hasten to recall, is by no means all negative so far as Bultmann is concerned, for it would seem to say that *his* is the way to the promised land; there is *no other*. Be this as it may, there have been numerous voices raised, in part, against Bultmann's choice of tools, in part relative to the structure he has raised with their use. To cite one example: Bishop J. A. T. Robinson in his *Honest to God* indicates three objections which he finds to Bultmann's work: first, Bultmann's "scientific dogmatism" and "air of old-fashioned modernism" as he constantly refers to "What 'no modern man' could accept"; second, the fact that for Bultmann "*so much* of the Gospel history" appears to be "expendable (e.g., the empty tomb *in toto*)," thus indicating that he is so very "distrustful of the tradition," though in fact "historical scepticism is not necessarily implied in his critique of mythology"; and third, "his heavy reliance on . . . Heidegger's Existentialism." The Bishop does not find this philosophy by any means to be "the only alternative" to the "mythological world-view" of the Bible, as Bultmann appears to suggest. (P. 35.)

In our attempt to evaluate Bultmann's image of the historical Jesus, we shall glance at once at both his tools and the results he has achieved with them, hoping by this method to conserve our space. And we shall proceed on a sort of principle of involution, looking first at the elements that are far away from the Christian context and then coming to observe his use of the Biblical materials. First, then, and perhaps farthest from the Biblical approach, is Bultmann's attachment for Heidegger's existentialism. This is a philosophy and *ipso facto* out of line with the Biblical categories, and therefore obviously not to be taken too seriously. Yet, Bultmann expects that we shall take it with sufficient seriousness to substitute an "existentialist eschatology" for the Bible's "mythological eschatology" as he conceives it. And, as we have seen, he finds this substitution present in the mind and teaching of

Jesus, in that he shows no interest in the history of his people or in that people's nearness to the eschatological drama, but only in each individual's confrontation by God's demand and Kingdom on his life.

Here, be it noted, we are again confronted with the typical German theologian's "either-or," and as before we must deny that such a dilemma exists, or perhaps better that the truth lies somewhere between the two focuses proposed. For, in the first place, if Jesus' teaching *is,* or may alternatively *be interpreted acceptably by,* an existentialist view of eschatology, then so is the prophetic teaching of the O.T. It is not true to say that Jesus introduced an existentialist view of God's demand on the individual that was unknown to the Hebrew prophets. Nor is it true to say that he abandoned an interest in the eschatology of the Nation (and/or all peoples) such as they accepted. The prophet Nathan's "You are the man," directed to King David after the recounting of the parable of the little ewe lamb, is as clear a case of confrontation as any in Scripture (II Sam. 12:1-14), and as likely an example of "existentialist eschatology." And this case can be duplicated almost time without number from the experiences or words of Elijah, Micaiah ben Imlah, and the writing prophets who for the expression of their confrontation invented the declaration "The word of the Lord came to. . . ." If Jesus speaks of an existential confrontation, so do these great men of God.

Likewise, Jesus does not ignore the group experience or that of the Nation or of all men at the end of history. Thus, Bornkamm finds it present in the Q (and M modification) saying at Luke 13:28-29 (‖ Matt. 8:11-12): "Many will come from east and west and sit at table with Abraham, Isaac, and Jacob in the kingdom of heaven" (BJN-67, 78). Moreover, that Jesus' eschatology is not exclusively individualistic (and so existentialist) is tacitly admitted by Bultmann himself when he accepts Jesus' reference to the "coming Son of man" (Mark 8:38; Matt. 24:27, 37, 44; Luke 11:30) without identifying this figure with himself (BNTTh-26, 28-30). That such a figure should at any time in the church's history, in view of Dan. 7:13 ff. and the "Similitudes" of the Book of Enoch (chs. 37 to 70), be thought a lonely one without followers or associates, whether at its *parousia* or any other period, is unthinkable. W. G. Kümmel, Bultmann's successor at Marburg, in a lengthy examination of Bultmann's suggestion relative to "the 'futurist' eschatology in Jesus' message," concludes that this cannot be given up even though it involves a "mythological form." His reason is that "this would result in a complete disintegration of Jesus' message that man through Jesus' appearance in the present is placed in a definite situation in the *history* of salvation advancing toward the end, and the figure and activity of Jesus would lose their fundamental character as the *historical* activity of the *God* who wishes to lead his kingdom upwards" (KPF-148).

It is this typical lack of interest in the *historical,* or even as we have seen Bultmann's wish to substitute *biography* for history in the universal sense, that appears so prominently among the existentialists and that the N.T. student finds he cannot accept. Not, certainly, as a trustworthy statement of the view of the N.T. as a whole and of Jesus' teaching in particular. For, throughout the Gospels, Jesus is portrayed as one who consciously appears at a particular point in the history of the "chosen people," announces the near coming of the Kingdom of God and in several passages speaks of its triumphant consummation. In spite, therefore, of what tradition may have done by way of enhancing certain features of his teaching and of the narra-

tive in connection with such events as the "triumphal
entry" and the "cleansing of the Temple," Bornkamm concludes that *"the struggle against the spiritual leaders of the
nation was thereby opened by himself"* (BJN-158, italics
added). Such a conclusion makes of Jesus a truly historical figure and one who is himself concerned about history's developments and who has a large share in God's purpose being consummated through it. Add to this Jesus'
undoubted interest in the individual and in his confrontation by the gospel and its claims on his life, which Bultmann proclaims with admirable vigor, and we see that as
between "existentialist eschatology" and "mythological eschatology," the case is not one of "either-or," but rather of
"both-and."

To much that is written regarding Jesus' teaching about
the consummation of the Kingdom, the present writer has
added his own conviction that even Mark, ch. 13, is essentially Jesus' own teaching. In this chapter and to a degree
in the parallels in Matthew and Luke, Jesus is truly represented as employing the language of apocalyptic against
the apocalyptists; it just begins to appear that the choice is
either in favor of this view or else that, with the majority
of N.T. scholars, the chapter is a bit of Jewish apocalyptic
later found acceptable by the church and so read back into
Jesus' mouth. If this view should be found correct, then
this chapter would, so to speak, place the capstone on
Jesus' interest in and pronouncement about the consummation of God's historical concern. (BIJ-56; BRM-245.)

Secondly, following the method of involution suggested,
one comes to Bultmann's study of the various ethnic
mythologies, a study that as we have just seen finds its
final conclusion as relates to Jesus and his teaching in the
suggestion that we must substitute an "existentialist eschatology" for the mythological one found throughout Scrip-

ture, and here Bultmann believes that Jesus himself has shown us the way. But the mythical element in the Gospels is by no means limited to the eschatological interest. We have already given as much space as we can allow for a glance at Bultmann's comprehensive coverage of the history of the oral tradition in the Synoptics, and have briefly mentioned his use of the phrase "Christ myth" and how through the Gospels this myth is imposed on the narrative. (BHST-Ch. II and 348; see also Appendix 3.) Once again, this is all in accord with Wrede's findings against which Schweitzer, as we have seen, waged strenuous warfare.

Here, then, space will be given to but two general observations on this subject. The first of these concerns is the fact that for the most part Biblical scholarship with scarcely a word of protest has shown itself prepared to employ the term "myth" of the relevant literary phenomenon found throughout Scripture. The justification for this that is usually cited lies in the fact that for the student of religion, *myth* is a story told about a divine person (or one thought to be divine) with a religious motivation and with no judgment expressed as to the story's historic validity. It is said that myth and parable are alike in this that the story involved teaches the religious or ethical lesson intended and that this is all that matters.

In the Scriptural context, this statement is without doubt true for the parable. But for the myth, it is open to question. Rather, it seems certain that the prophetic writers of Scripture, in view of their extraordinay emphasis on the historical and its necessary validity, made a distinction here. Comparison with the Near East "creation myths" and others of like nature, *when employed by the prophetic authors of Scripture or its sources, appears to suggest that these writers demythicized their source mate-*

rials before employing them. What we have in Scripture, therefore, is the prophetic endeavor to achieve the result that Bultmann aims at. No doubt it is not always as thorough a success as we should wish, but at least the effort appears to have been made and in general it is only the scholar with his fastidious efforts who is able to discover the mythical elements that still remain.

Again, for the average reader of Scripture the use of the term "myth" is misleading in the extreme. For the English reader, at all events, a myth is *ipso facto* nonhistorical and the adjective *"mythical" means untrue.* In India, this writer, together with a colleague, was once challenged to debate the proposition—"Resolved that Jesus Christ was a myth." Our challenger was a Hindu pandit who had been reading Robertson and Drews and others in the "mythical school." It was obvious that he meant—*Jesus Christ was not a historical person.* Had we challenged him to come back next day and debate before the same Aryah Somaj audience in their *mandir* the like proposition—"Resolved that Lord Krishna was a myth," he and his colleagues would have laughed us to scorn. This, for the simple reason that to his sophisticated sort of Hinduism, which is a monistic philosophy, the proposition would hold neither meaning nor importance. He knew quite well that for a historically grounded faith such as that of the Bible, the historical validity of the Gospel account of Jesus Christ did matter. Hence, his challenge!

Doubtless the criteria of the average reader of the Scriptures are not to be accepted at face value by the scholar. But, when such criteria express a real difference of great import that serve to define or set off religions, philosophies, or theologies from one another, and when moreover a genuine concern for such differentia appears to be found among the writers of Scripture themselves, then one imagines some cognizance should be taken of the matter. In fact, it is for these reasons, I submit, that so much scholarly conversation has been stirred up by Bultmann's pronouncements on the subject. Bultmann's term "Christ myth" serves to state a valid difference between the views of Wrede which he inherited, on the one hand, and those of Schweitzer on the other.

Thirdly and finally, as to Bultmann's handling of the Gospel accounts as a result both of his allegiance to the usual solution of the Synoptic problem and of his thorough analysis of the sources in the form of oral tradition (form criticism), we shall have to content ourselves by examining but one item at this point, allowing this examination to stand as an example of a procedure to be followed through as relentlessly as Bultmann's work is itself. "Bultmann among modern scholars," this writer has stated in the revision of *Peake's Commentary on the Bible,* "has committed himself to the assertion that the three predictions of Jesus' passion and resurrection are *vaticinia ex eventu,* on the ground that the source common to Mt. and Lk. (Q) does not contain these predictions (cf. R. Bultmann, *Theology of the NT* (1951), i., 30).

"The argument, however, overlooks the fact that the source Q contains no reference whatever to Jesus' passion either as prediction or as historic event. Surely the author of this source knew of Jesus' passion as event! It seems obvious, therefore, that his lack of any reference to the passion is due to his interest for the moment lying in another direction. The account of Peter's 'rebuke' of Jesus' reference to his anticipated passion and of our Lord's answering rebuttal of Peter in the strongest terms is our best guarantee of the genuineness of these predictions. In the Fourth Gospel the role played by Peter on the occasion of the feet-washing in the Upper Room is the counterpart of his attitude on this occasion (Jn 13:6-10).

"It seems strange that Bultmann should be concerned to deny Jesus' insight at this point. For no-one has given stronger expression to the prophetic character of Jesus' teaching than he. Nor has anyone stated in clearer terms the essential unity of the eschatological and ethical elements in the teaching of Jesus. 'Both things,' he remarks, 'the eschatological proclamation and the ethical demand, direct man to the fact that he is thereby brought before God, that God stands before him; both direct him into his Now as the hour of decision for God' (ibid., 21). If these things be true for man generally, are they not also true for Jesus? And can it be that with all his prophetic insight, his understanding of human nature, his observation of the fickleness of the crowds as they begin to count the cost of discipleship, his certain knowledge of the hostility of the religious authorities, yet Jesus does not foresee for himself that this is his hour of decision and of reckoning? Indeed, had the gospels not recorded such insight on the part of our Lord, certainly we should have had to infer it!" (P. 741.)

3

The Essene-like "Teacher
of Righteousness"

In the spring of 1948, the present writer published a volume entitled *The Religion of Maturity* in which, along with the Christian faith, he treated certain phases of Judaism as it existed and flourished at the beginning of the Christian era. He said, however, that he would "eliminate treatment of the minor Jewish sects" (BRM-8n). Among these he included "the Zealots, Essenes, . . . (and) Therapeutae." The book was outdated before it issued from the press, to which it was submitted the very month (February, 1947) in which the "Dead Sea Scrolls" came to the attention of Western scholarship! The only excuse for such a mistake must be that at that date every Biblical scholar would have agreed that, so far as there was any evidence at the time, the sect of the Essenes at least was *culturally ineffective* in Jesus' day.

Having said so much about scholarly *opinion* of a quarter century ago, however, the writer should perhaps add just a further word indicative of the *alertness* of Biblical scholarship. For in the volume referred to above, he did make some reference to the only fragment known at the time to be Essene, viz., the "Zadokite Fragment" (now known as the Damascus Document, found in the Cairo Geniza and edited by Solomon Schechter in 1910. From

this early find, we were already acquainted with the
Essene teaching about the "Teacher of Righteousness,"
the "lay Messiah" (Messiah of Israel) and "priestly
Messiah" (Messiah of Aaron)—whether one or two
figures is still in dispute, as well as with many of the sect's
views on theological and ethical subjects. And the writer
had remarked, "Of all the priestly literature extant, both
canonical and extracanonical, this fragment is undoubtedly closest to the teaching of the New Testament."
(BRM-110.) Then, after making a somewhat detailed
study of the fragment covering several pages, he
concluded, "By these and other like emphases the Zadokite Fragment succeeds in creating an atmosphere which is
nearer in spirit to the teaching of Jesus than either is to
that of Mishnah or Talmud" (BRM-119). One may be allowed perhaps to observe that this early judgment has
been more than corroborated by the later remarkable finds
at Khirbet Qumran.

Now, however, the problem emerges whether Jesus' relationship with the Qumran community may not have
been far more intimate than the present writer intended in
the above quotations. And almost as soon as the scrolls
discovered from 1947 onward in the various caves and
more recently even at Masada were made known to Jewish and Christian scholars, the thought was advanced that
in one way or another such a relationship must have existed. As a result much has been written pro and con on
the subject. It has been suggested in some quarters that
John the Baptist was probably raised as an orphan by the
Qumran Essenes and that he may have later taught in the
monastery at Khirbet Qumran, that Jesus himself spent
some time there and was indoctrinated with the Essene
views, that Luke's "great many of the priests" (Acts 6:7)
who became Christians would probably be Qumran

priests, and in general that there must have been many spiritual and theological contacts between the sect and the Jewish Church at Jerusalem in the early days.

This is obviously not the place to discuss this group of ideas. We are constrained by the goal we have set forth in this book merely to deal with two of three authors who believe that Jesus of Nazareth was so far influenced by the Essene views regarding the coming deliverer of Israel as to endeavor to fulfill the image of that "coming one" as his lifework.

Two scholars particularly have taken advanced points of view in the matter and for the most part we shall limit our discussion to their positions. The earlier of these to write was the French Catholic, A. Dupont-Sommer, whose views are conveniently set out in his book entitled *The Jewish Sect of Qumran and the Essenes* (1955). Taking his stance on what is said in the two Qumran scrolls known as the "Habbakuk commentary" and the "Testament of Levi" (one of the series known to scholars as the "Testaments of the Twelve Patriarchs"), this author believes that the great Essene figure known as the "Teacher of Righteousness" dates from the first third of the first century B.C. He was, according to Dupont-Sommer, the "leader and reformer of the Sect of the Covenant, was persecuted by the Highpriest Aristobulus II, and was punished and put to death by him" (DJSQ-49).

But the Messianic or New Age will see the coming of a "new Priest." Who, then, we may ask, is this figure? Our author replies, "the Teacher of Righteousness himself"; for, "after his earthly career and his ignominious death, he is now to be seen translated to an eschatological plane, invested with full Messianic glory, and enthroned as chief of the new universe. 'Saviour of the World'—that is how

Chapters X and XIV of the Testament of Levi describe him" (DJSQ-52 f.).

In addition to this outstanding figure in the scrolls, however, there are two others of comparable importance. These are the two known rather generally as "Messiah (or Anointed) of Aaron/Levi" and "Messiah (or Anointed) of Israel/Judah." Of these figures, Dupont-Sommer writes, "When the Teacher of Righteousness was converted into a Messiah, the two attributes previously distinct, the Anointed of Levi and the Anointed of Judah, were transferred to him in one and the same person" (DJSQ-53). Hence, another scroll, "the Damascus Document uses exclusively the term 'Anointed of Aaron and Israel'" (DJSQ-54).

It is not difficult to see how the equation Teacher of Righteousness = coming "New Priest" = Messiah = Savior of the World may be said to have created a pattern for anyone such as Jesus, if sufficiently steeped in such teaching and convinced of his own divine call, to have followed. And this, indeed, is generally the conclusion at which John Allegro has long since arrived and the thesis that he is well known for seeking to defend. He has done this both in scholarly publications and in the more popular media of press and broadcast (BBC). He has also been answered after both fashions by colleagues and a superior (H. H. Rowley). Some of the more popular reports of the controversy thus aroused may be seen in *Time*, for Feb. 6 and April 2, 1956, and in *Harper's Magazine* for August and October, 1966. We shall largely limit our discussion of his views to his most complete statement as found in ADSS and ASOC, and as comparison of the two reveals this to be the same book throughout, we shall further limit our examination of Allegro's position to the later edition of the work (ASOC), as it appears under the title *The Dead Sea Scrolls and the Origins of Christianity.*

ALLEGRO'S VIEWS ON JESUS' RELATION TO QUMRAN

With a view to elaborating Allegro's thesis on the part the Essene teachings played in Jesus' activities and aims, we shall indicate briefly:

First, his interpretation of the part the great figures mentioned in the various scrolls took or were prophesied as about to take in the community's life and in the final age. There is, of course, the "Teacher of Righteousness" whom we have already mentioned. Allegro believes this figure whose personal name was probably "Zadok" (ASOC-95), as the sect called themselves or, at least, their clerical order *"bene* Zadok" (sons of Zadok), lived during the reign of the Hasmonean priest-king, Alexander Jannaeus (104-78 B.C.). This character he would identify in turn with the "Lion of Wrath" referred to in the sect's *Commentary on the Book of Nahum* (2:12), or the "Wicked Priest" in its *Commentary on the Book of Habbakuk* (2:7) (ASOC-95 f.).

This "Lion of Wrath" or "Wicked Priest," now to be identified with Alexander Jannaeus, according to the Nahum commentary on one occasion hung his enemies up alive. This incident Allegro equates with Josephus' account in *Antiquities,* XIII, 14.2, to the effect that Alexander Jannaeus, while "feasting with his concubines, in the sight of all the city," had Jews who had dared to fight against him to the number of "about eight hundred of them to be crucified; and while they were living, he ordered the throats of their children and wives to be cut before

their eyes" (ASOC-98-100). In his more recent statements and by implication in ASOC (148 f.), Allegro
suggests that the Teacher of Righteousness suffered
crucifixion at the hands of this wicked priest-king and
would come again after being resurrected as the "Last
Priest" or "Messiah of Levi," when "a general resurrection"
would also occur (ASOC-149).

At the same time, however, our author does not equate
the two expected Messiahs of the Qumran sect after the
manner of Dupont-Sommer. These, he thinks rather, were
separate—a priestly and a lay Messiah, much after the
fashion of the "Aaronic High Priest and the Davidic
prince" of Zech. 4:14; and he adds that in other literature
also the two were consistently kept separate. The case of
El'azar the High Priest and Shim'on bar Kochebah, the
Prince of Israel, at the time of the 2d Jewish War of A.D.
132-135 is a case in point. (ASOC-150.)

Secondly, in any event, it seems clear that much that
had been gleaned from the scrolls by way either of direct
statement or of inference is suggestive of the relevance of
such materials as background for the New Testament's
account of Jesus of Nazareth, his life and ministry. This
point Allegro develops in the last three chapters of his
book, particularly in the last chapter entitled "The Qumran Sect and Jesus" (ASOC-155-162). Comparing the
Qumran scrolls with the New Testament writings, Allegro
finds many suggestive likenesses between them at vital
points. Especially is this the case when one looks at what
is said of the experiences of and prophecies about Jesus,
on the one hand, and the "Teacher of Righteousness,"
the "Messiah of Israel," and the "Messiah of Aaron," on
the other.

Thus, in the "Last Days," the Teacher of Righteousness
was to receive "vindication" as "the perfect mediator be-

tween Man and God" (ASOC-149). This would occur in
the "new Kingdom" or "New Jerusalem," the "new, spiritual Canaan" where through the mediatorship of the
Teacher (who was also the "priestly Messiah"), "communion with God would be complete" for the members of the
Essene community (ASOC-149). Points of contact here
with the early church's teachings are too obvious to require specific reference and our author gives none.

But it is particularly with the "Davidic Messiah" (Messiah of Israel) "that we may expect to find correspondence
with Christian ideas" (ASOC-151). And such proves, indeed, to be the case. For, this Messiah is represented as "a
war leader and judge" (ASOC-150), who in the *Manual*
is said to "[. . . smite the peoples] with the might of thy
[mouth]," even as in II Thess. 2:8 it is said of Jesus that
he will "kill the wicked with the breath of his lips"
(ASOC-151). Moreover, there is a similarity between the
inscription on Jesus' cross ("King of the Jews") and the
title of "Prince of Israel" which is really what this Qumran
Messiah's title means. Again, in Isa., ch. 11, it is said that
the coming leader in Israel will be a "shoot out of the stock
of Jesse" and in Deut. 18:18 that he will be "the 'Prophet' ";
and both of these prophecies are applied to Jesus, on the
one hand, and to the Qumran Messiah of Israel, on the
other (ASOC-152). Similarly, the prophecy in II Samuel
7:14 to the effect that God would be to the offspring of
David as "his father, and he shall be my son" was applied
to both figures in Qumran scrolls and New Testament
(ASOC-152). And the same may be said of the use of
Zech. 9:9, which is applied to the triumphal entry (so-
called) of Jesus into Jerusalem, and is found to be "de-
pendent upon a messianic interpretation of Gen. 49:10, 11,
about the Lion of Judah," a passage given a messianic interpretation at Qumran. The "coronation Psalm 45" is

also used of both Jesus and the Messiah of Israel (ASOC-152, 153). (Note that the case in this paragraph has purposely been stated vaguely and without specific references; this is in imitation of Allegro's loose argument at this point. There is no reason to further his argument by giving the proper references when he does not!)

This same loose method of arguing without citations characterizes the chapter on "The Qumran Sect and Jesus" in which Allegro's major presentation of his case relating Jesus with Qumran is found. There is not a single citation to the Qumran scrolls in the chapter and but one (Acts 6:7) to the New Testament. We shall simply summarize his main points, therefore, as clearly as possible and without the required references to either corpus of writings.

Jesus' period of temptation in the desert not far from Khirbet Qumran is, our author holds, "the key to the whole life and teaching of Jesus" and "our first concrete correspondence" between Jesus and the desert community (ASOC-155). In suffering this, Jesus, like the sect, "is identifying himself with the True Israel" and through tribulation endeavoring to bring about "atonement for the world's sins" (ASOC-156). Allegro does not hesitate to see Jesus as one who consciously is assuming the role of the Isaianic Suffering Servant in thus suffering as one of the righteous remnant. The Qumran sect had so visualized their own role in a corporate capacity even as Jesus was now doing in his individual one. And both he and they were resisting the wiles of the Devil in order to bring in "the new Age and God's Kingdom." What Jesus and the sect were both doing was fighting the ecumenical battle of "Good against Evil" and this was a battle to be won for "all mankind" (ASOC-157).

Hence, Jesus' appeal—"The time is fulfilled, and the

kingdom of God is at hand," as we find in Mark's Gospel. In the end he knew there would be "an ignominious death" for himself, but this did not disturb him, "for that had been there from the beginning." What did disturb Jesus was his realization that there would be many who would not heed the call. Yet he went resolutely on with his message of "impending doom" and his acts were all performed in accordance with his central aim; thus, the feeding of the thousands was "a rehearsal of the Messianic Banquet," his mighty works proof of the "victory of Light over Darkness," and the like (ASOC-158).

Like the Qumran Essenes, Jesus had only "contempt" for the authorities in Jerusalem. "Hypocrisy" was his main charge against them; the harlots and sinners he could love, but the "self-righteous" he could only criticize and despise. The "legalism" of the Pharisees, for example, had led them to overlook the real battle that must be drawn between the "powers of darkness" and the "forces of light." This, both Jesus and the Qumran community sensed as the religious powers in Jewry did not (ASOC-159). Basically the apocalyptic message of the Essenes and the "homely preaching" of Jesus in his parables is the same (ASOC-160).

The question arises how Jesus got in contact with the sect, inasmuch as no evidence of his being a member of the monastic Qumran community exists. The answer, Allegro believes, is to be found in the fact that contemporary testimony indicates many Essenes to have lived "in the towns and villages" of the land (ASOC-161). Jesus will thus have come to know them and to acquaint himself with their teachings. And so we may conclude that "both groups" (that is, the Qumran community and "the Jewish-Christian Church" of the earliest period) must have been "part of the same religious movement"

(ASOC-161). The fundamental difference between them would appear to be that one like Paul, for example, found his "faith hinged on an historical Resurrection of Jesus," while "the Covenanters were presumably still waiting for the Resurrection of their Master" when disaster overcame them and bore them away in A.D. 70 (ASOC-162).

IS ALLEGRO'S "DAVIDIC MESSIAH" THE PROTOTYPE OF THE REAL JESUS?

With a view to acquainting the reader in advance with an estimate of Allegro's views on the part of what is no doubt the group best qualified to express such an estimate, we quote here from the letter written to the London *Times* for March 16, 1956, by his colleagues in the "Scrollery" in Jerusalem. This group was an international team appointed to edit and publish the manuscripts found in Cave IV. The entire team consisted of eight members, as follows: Fathers D. Barthèlemy and Jean Starcky of France, Father J. T. Milik of Poland, Dr. Claus-Hunno Hunziger of Germany, Monsignor Patrick W. Skehan and Frank M. Cross, Jr., of America, and John Strugnell and John Allegro of England. Most or all of this team have since become well known for their publications relative to the finds at Khirbet Qumran and related areas. Allegro gives some very good photographs of this team at work (see ASOC-200, 201, 204, 212).

After his return to England, having done a stint in the "Scrollery," Allegro gave three broadcasts over the BBC to acquaint the layman generally with what had been found in the scrolls. His revelations proved so startling that the international team, or that portion of it at the time at work in the "Scrollery," decided to drop everything and go over all the as-yet-unpublished scrolls to which their colleague had made reference as containing his new finds. As a result they wrote and sent to the *Times* the letter referred to, in which they said: "There are no unpublished texts at the disposal of Mr. Allegro other than those of which the originals are at present in the Palestine Archaeological Museum where we are working. Upon the appearance in the press of citation from Mr. Allegro's broadcasts we have reviewed all the pertinent materials, published and unpublished. We are unable to see in the text the 'findings' of Mr. Allegro. We find no crucifixion of the 'teacher,' no deposition from the cross, and no 'broken body of their Master' to be stood guard over until Judgment Day. . . . It is our conviction that either he has misread the texts or he has built up a chain of conjectures which the materials do not support."

Those signing this letter included Jean Starcky, J. T. Milik, Patrick W. Skehan, and John Strugnell of the team, and also Roland de Vaux, Director of the École Biblique et Archéologique Française in Jerusalem, a scholar of great distinction who has worked on the scrolls from the beginning. Meanwhile, some of the unpublished manuscripts, mostly fragmentary in the extreme, to which Allegro referred, have come out in print (that is, both in the original text and in translation). *The Dead Sea Scriptures* (1964), edited by Theodor H. Gaster, in its revised form contains a sufficient number of them for the layman to examine intelligently on his own. Others have been given considerable coverage in technical journals and are known to all scholars working in the field. Many if not all of these have disputed with Allegro respecting the proper conclusions to be drawn from these data.

The reader must realize that in the case of the Dead Sea Scrolls we are dealing with an enormous library containing hundreds, if not thousands, of different books and these in many manuscripts differing from one another. Writing in 1960, Frank M. Cross, Jr., a member as above indicated of the team working on the Cave IV collection, estimated that 382 manuscripts from this cave alone had been identified. Of these and other manuscripts in this cave, some "tens of thousands of fragments" have been collected. It is these which constitute the problem to be worked over by the international team mentioned (see Frank M. Cross, Jr., *The Ancient Library of Qumran,* 1961), and the corpus at which they have been working from Cave IV probably constituted "the great library once housed in the Essene community center" (CALQ-34). It should be obvious, then, that to become impatient at the seeming slowness with which such effort involving paleographical, linguistic, photographic, and numerous other skills is achieved is unreasonable. As Cross comments relative to the thousands of fragments involved, "This is the ultimate in jigsaw puzzles" (CALQ-38)! It is equally unscientific to jump to hasty conclusions suggested by a cursory examination of the evidence presented by such a mass of materials.

In view of the magnitude of the problem, this short chapter can merely provide *a brief checklist* for the reader's interest and possible guidance in reaching something like a fair estimate of the value of Dupont-Sommer's and Allegro's conclusions.

1. Let the reader inquire into the matter of the proper identification of the great figures involved in the scrolls and of the historical situation(s) indicated. Dupont-Sommer and Allegro do not agree on these identifications. The latter thinks the Teacher of Righteousness was a man named Zadok and that the Lion of Wrath or Wicked Priest was Alexander Jannaeus (104-78 B.C.); the for-

mer, arguing that the Teacher was "the leader and reformer" of the Essene community, places him under the
Hasmonean priest-king Aristobulus II at about 65 B.C.
Again, Frank Cross, who has been called "the foremost
authority on the Dead Sea Scrolls," identifies the Teacher
with an unknown priest "presumably of Zadokite lineage"
who flourished in all likelihood from the end of the priest-
king Jonathan's reign (160-142 B.C.), into that of Simon
(142-135 B.C.), suffering persecution and defeat perhaps
under more than one of these Hasmonean rulers (CALQ-
156). Cross, then, would identify the Wicked Priest or
Lion of Wrath not with Alexander Jannaeus or Aristobulus II, but with the earlier Simon. Matthew Black (*The
Scrolls and Christian Origins,* 1961) would push the
origins of the sect back still earlier to the reign of Antio-
chus IV (Epiphanes), whom he identifies with the Wicked
Priest (175-163 B.C.), the Teacher, in this case, being the
high priest Onias III (p. 20). Still other identifications
have been proposed, on the basis of both the internal evidence of the scrolls and the contemporary history as
known from Biblical and extra-Biblical sources.

For our purposes, these identifications are important if
we are to hope to find a character in pre-Christian times
who might conceivably serve as an exemplar or prototype
for Jesus as the crucified and risen, or even as a persecuted, Messiah. After devoting some fifty pages of closely
packed citations to ancient and current literature with a
view to making these identifications, Cross, for example, is
forced to conclude, "While the Wicked Priest attempted to
take his rival's life, the Righteous Teacher was spared,
perhaps to be killed later by another adversary, perhaps to
die of old age" (CALQ-158), and he is inclined to com-
pare the work of the Teacher to that of Moses rather than
to that of Jesus (CALQ-160).

2. Another crucial question along the same lines concerns the identification of the historical Teacher of Righteousness with the coming "New Priest" or "Last Priest" and both with a to-be-resurrected "Messiah of Aaron/ Levi" (see above). Such identification is made by both Dupont-Sommer and Allegro and denied by equally competent scholarship. Much depends on our understanding of two famous passages from the Damascus Document. These read: "From the day the Teacher of the community died until the Messiahs of Aaron and Israel arise" (19:34) and "until the Teacher of Righteousness arises in the end of days" (6:11). Inferences that may be made here are obvious. But they remain inferences, and Cross comments, "If the Essenes did expect their Teacher to return as the priestly Messiah, they have been exceedingly indirect in expressing their hope." (CALQ-229.) Contrariwise, as he further observes, "the N.T. preoccupation with the death and Messiahship of Jesus is in significant contrast" (CALQ-229).

3. Still another problem of significance for the Christian faith concerns the possible association of Qumran's Messiah(s) with the "Suffering Servant" concept found in Deutero-Isaiah, and even with the Danielic "Son of Man" (Dan. 7:13 ff.). If such Servant passages as Isa., ch. 53, were to be associated with one or other Messiah in the scrolls, then a redemptive function on the part of that figure might readily be established.

In the Thanksgiving Hymns of Qumran, *the poet* does employ language suggestive of the Servant; he even calls *himself* in addressing God, "Thy servant" (9:10), saying, "Through me hast Thou illumined the faces of full many" (4:27), and "I am a source of healing unto them that repent" (2:8), and the like. But there is no association of this sufferer *with either Messiah* in these or other Hymns.

Similarly, the Hymns contain language suggestive of Isa. 7:14 ("a young woman shall conceive and bear a son"; cf. "And I was in distress as a woman in travail, bringing forth her first-born," Hymn 3:7) and Isa. 9:6 ("his name . . . Wonderful Counselor"; cf. "A Wondrous Counsellor in his might," Hymn 3:10).

As M. Black remarks, however, about this latter passage, "it is not of the birth of any particular individual of which the author is speaking, but of the birth of a whole community of people" (op. cit., p. 150). And there need be no doubt that the same is true of the "Sufferer" passage above. In any case, *in neither passage does the author of the Hymns relate the character he is describing with either Qumran Messiah.* So, we may perhaps not unadvisedly conclude this section with the summary which Cross presents at this point. "Nowhere at Qumran, at least so far, is there a hint of 'highest' New Testament Christology: the pre-existence of the Messiah, the Second Adam, the Son of Man." (CALQ-221.)

4. In concluding this discussion of a most complex series of data arising from the finds at Khirbet Qumran, the writer wishes to suggest that there is a certain similarity between the sect's use of the terms and ideas associated with the figures of the Teacher and the Messiah(s), and that of the Targum of Jonathan bar Uzziel at Isa., ch. 53, in approaching the work of the Servant. *Alone among pre-Christian Jewish literary creations, this Aramaic Targum appears to endeavor to equate the Servant with the expectant Messiah.* But, when the author (translator, to be sure, from the Hebrew into the Aramaic of the day) came to vs. 3 ff. in which the afflictions of the Servant are mentioned, he transferred these to the people of Israel! Only the redemptive significance attaching to his "intercession" (v. 12) is allowed to stand to his credit. There can be little

doubt that *the later Christian idea of a Suffering Servant, even Crucified, Messiah (I Cor. 1:23) is as much as "stumbling block" to this translator* as it was in the days of the early church for the Jews generally, as Paul remarks. *The same attitude appears to characterize the Qumran scrolls*; so that among this monastic Essene community, as among all pre-Christian Jews, there is *no clear acceptance of the concept of a Suffering Servant, Messiah.*

4

The Nazorean Scheming Messiah

Hugh J. Schonfield's *The Passover Plot* (1966) is the only book in our series written by a member of the Jewish faith and a practicing Jew, but it is the fourth meriting the accolade "Jewish." To arrive at an understanding of this author's thesis, it is necessary to place side by side several definitive statements he makes. After a rather complicated skein of ideas has been simplified, as far as this may be done without harm to the whole, the ideas with which he is attempting to deal include the following: first, Jesus believed "that he was the expected Messiah of Israel" (SPP-14); secondly, Jesus was "a master of his destiny, expecting events to conform to the requirements of prophetic intimations, contriving those events when necessary, contending with friends and foes to ensure that the predictions would be fulfilled" (SPP-15); thirdly, such "mastery" on Jesus' part demanded of him "the most careful scheming and plotting" with a view to achieving the prophecies of Scripture relative to the Messiah (SPP-132), including his understanding that "he was to suffer on the cross, but not to perish on it" and therefore to "make what provision he could for his survival" (SPP-162). "Jesus," accordingly, "contrived to give the impression of death" (SPP-163) by having administered to him

"a drug" that had a soporific effect (SPP-166 f.). Thereafter he had arranged that Joseph of Arimathea should
have him quickly removed to his own tomb where he
could be speedily revived (SPP-163-168). Unfortunately,
however, the Roman soldier pierced his side, and it may
have been this that completely spoiled the plan for Jesus
to be revived and resulted in his hasty reburial elsewhere
(SPP-168, 172).

Such is Schonfield's thesis insofar as he deals specifically with Jesus and his ultimate purpose for his lifework.
There is, however, at every point throughout the book a
sort of *overtone* that carries us beyond the author's immediate objective and, as it were, motivates his point of view
as a writer sharing a Jewish rather than a Christian outlook. It is important to indicate at the start what this overtone is, and in searching for a clear statement of it, one
imagines that the following passage contains its gist:

"Christians," Schonfield writes, "continue to be troubled
today by the Church's contradictory doctrines, which
arose from the unhappy endeavour to blend incompatible
Pagan and Jewish ideas." He does not intend, he remarks,
to go into the minutiae of these doctrines. Rather he pro-
poses merely to point out that the Christian faith began
as a "messianic movement" that arose within Judaism at
a "critical moment" and that, as it developed, it departed
from its fountainhead in Judaism in proportion as it
went out into the pagan world. This fact "conditioned"
its development in the direction of paganism, though the
faith continued to retain some of the "marks of its ances-
try." Under "alien ideas and modes of thought" it eventually departed so far from its origins as to cease to be
"a reliable guide to its own beginnings." So our task—one
attended with "enormous difficulty"—is to endeavor to
discover the "relics of the primitive period" that may have

survived throughout Christianity's vast changes under the
stimulus of "fresh circumstances" (SPP-204, 205).

What we have termed the "overtone" in Schonfield's
book is as important perhaps as his immediate thesis for
the future of the Christian faith, and we imagine that most
Biblical scholars would agree that it can find better docu-
mentation than the thesis. For this author assumes, as the
above statement shows, that the phrase "messianic movement" can mean but one thing, that this must be defined in
terms of first-century Jewish ideas, that what is non-
Jewish is necessarily "Pagan," and that it can be only
"fresh circumstances" and not fresh illumination that
would lead the church to adopt what Schonfield believes
to be "alien ideas and modes of thought." This "overtone"
is, on the surface at any rate, so very convincing, so very
pat, that one is reminded of what used to be termed "the
assured results of Biblical criticism"; certainly if there are
"assured results," Schonfield's "overtone" answers to the
demands and may be so labeled.

But the work of much Biblical scholarship during the
last quarter century has, as so often before, called such results in question. Let us look briefly at but two champions
on the other side of this *Jewish versus Hellenistic nexus of
ideas.* Oscar Cullmann, writing in the *Journal of Biblical
Literature,* December, 1955, an article entitled "The Significance of the Qumran Texts for Research Into the Beginnings of Christianity," remarked: "We must view the
entire question of Hellenism vs. Judaism from a different
perspective than has become habitual. In the past, as soon
as Hellenistic influences could be shown in a N.T. writing,
the immediate conclusion was: This must have been written very late. The Gospel of John is a case in point. Since
Hellenistic elements are found in the Gospel, it was believed that a very late origin was proved. Behind this false

conclusion stood a false, or at least too schematic, conception of the origin of Christianity, namely, the idea that at first Christianity was merely Jewish, and then later became Hellenistic. This basic error led to a whole series of further errors." (Pp. 213 f.) The relevance of this quotation and its flat contradiction of Schonfield's assumption (his overtone) is obvious.

Much more recently, Cyrus H. Gordon in his *The Common Background of Greek and Hebrew Civilizations* (1965) has gone farther, developing the thesis contained in his title. His entire book must be read and digested in order to experience the impact which it is highly qualified to make. A single quotation here must suffice to show the relation of his argument to the problem before us. He writes: "The prevailing attitude (which is gradually losing its grip) may be described as the tacit assumption that ancient Israel and Greece are two water-tight compartments, totally different from each other. One is said to be sacred; the other, profane; one, Semitic; the other, Indo-European. One, Asiatic and Oriental; the other, European and Occidental. But the fact is that both flourished during the same centuries, in the same East Mediterranean corner of the globe, with both ethnic groups in contact with each other from the start." (P. 11.) In his even later *Ugarit and Minoan Crete* (1966), Professor Gordon, writing along similar lines, remarks, "But the Ugaritic epics, as will appear below, have unmistakable and organic parallels that link the pre-prophetic Hebrews with the prephilosophical Greeks." (P. 14.)

In the context of this fresh treatment of the interaction of Hebrew and Hellene, one would wish also to raise the question *de novo* already hinted at in the Introduction above relative to whether one may speak at all of a Jewish-Christian tradition. In the context of Schonfield's thought, I would phrase the problem so: Was the Judaism contemporary with Jesus in any of its forms true to the "faith of the fathers," that is, to the highest reach of the Hebrew prophets in their universalism, their extreme humanitarianism, their fine emphasis upon persons rather than on institutions, and the like? If not, then are we to attribute Christianity's absorption of this spirit of the prophets to the Hellenistic Church and not to Jesus himself, to the very "pagan" atmosphere into which the church after Jesus penetrated, to what Schonfield calls "fresh circumstances" in the Hellenistic world rather than to the same Spirit of the Living God that had led the prophets of old? For the moment, we are content to indicate the nature of the problem that Schonfield's overtone raises; perhaps on later pages we may come closer to suggesting its solution.

To come now to Schonfield's more immediate thesis relative to Jesus' possible Messiahship, his book is remarkable for the certainty with which it exhibits his belief that we may know the mind of the historic Jesus on the point. Here, the writer confesses to considerable relief, for this has been his own contention for a quarter century. Since the work of the first form critics in the early decades of the century, it has been popular to assume that, in view of the fact that it was the church that wrote our Gospels, further that it wrote them in a quite other *Sitz im Leben* than that experienced by Jesus, and still further that meanwhile the early witnesses had all been eliminated by the First Jewish War of A.D. 66-70, accompanied by the destruction, not alone of Jerusalem but also and particularly of the Jewish Christianity to which we have just made reference, therefore, the Gospels are all of a kind of opaque glass through which and around which we cannot hope to peer and so recover the image of the historic Jesus. This sort of extreme skepticism, one is happy to record, is not to be found anywhere in Schonfield's book. Rather, from beginning to end, it is replete with confident assertions of Jesus' views, his plans, his goals and his endeavors to achieve these. This makes, to say the least, refreshing reading, whether one is prepared or not to accept the author's own findings.

THE PLOT BEGINS TO THICKEN

In the development of his thesis, Schonfield somewhat vehemently denies that the Jews of the first Christian century were looking for a "Warrior Messiah," that is, one whose main objective would be the unsettling of the political rulers under whom they lived (SPP-34). The image of the Messiah looked for was rather to be understood in terms of Isa. 11:4, that is, as the quotation suggests, a Messiah characterized by "justice and righteousness" (see also S. of Sol. 17:28-31, 35-42; Ps. 45:7; 40:7-8). This was a spiritual Messiah with nationalistic implications, but no warrior as such. Further, according to this author, no other interpretation of the term "Messiah" may be entertained as being intelligible or permissible for Jesus' Jewish hearers, for they knew the prophetic requirements attaching to the term and would have rejected him had any other definition been proposed (SPP-21).

It is true, Schonfield concedes, that among the "peasantry of Palestine" there were those who believed in a crude, warlike sort of Messiah, but the Messiah concept is not to be judged through the eyes of such as they (SPP-35). He also allows that the appellative assigned to Jesus of "the Nazorean" (from *nezer,* branch, sprout) connects him with "an ancient Israelitish type of religion persisting in Galilee" (SPP-39 and Part Two, Ch. 2, 207 ff.). In

Galilee, he holds, it was permissible to join the Messianic
hope with those of the Suffering Just One and the "ideal
Israelite, the Son of Man" (SPP-40). This means, of
course, that as a Galilean, Jesus would be prepared to
adopt these ideas (Messiah, Suffering Servant, Son of
Man) for himself. That Jesus did all this, he believes, is
clear (SPP-14).

Further, Schonfield accepts this sort of Messiah-Jesus
on his own part and he has written a very fine chapter to
say as much—a confession as it were of his personal faith
(SPP-Part One, Ch. 14). In developing this thesis about
Jesus' conception of his own Messiahship, Schonfield
quotes with great appreciation Sir Edwyn Hoskyns and
Noel Davey's *The Riddle of the New Testament* (1931),
a book that to some extent follows the line laid down long
before by Albert Schweitzer (Chapter 1, above), to the
effect that as Messiah, Jesus believed "he must journey to
Jerusalem in order to be rejected and to die" (SPP-44).
Accepting this view of Jesus, Schonfield asks why we
should not see Jesus preparing a sort of "blueprint of the
Messiah's mission" which he intended to carry through to
the letter, not as a game to be played, but rather one about
which he was "in deadly earnest" (SPP-46). This was all
the more acceptable to Jesus as relating to himself, since
he shared the views of those in his day who saw the "Woes
of the Last Times" as already accomplished, particularly
in view of the extravagances of torture inflicted by Herod
the Great and the Roman overlords. The Qumran sect saw
these same events taking place and called them "the Period of the Wrath" (SPP-29-32).

It will now be instructive to follow Schonfield's development of his thesis of Jesus as the Jewish Messiah with the
straightforward chronological method he employs. In the
first place, it should be noted that there were "formative

years" behind what we may term Jesus' "call" to his divinely appointed task (SPP-58-69). During this period of preparation, he came to know that God had chosen him to fulfill what he "had inspired his messengers," the prophets, to set forth relative to the Messiah's task (SPP-68). Meanwhile and until the appointed time, "he could only prepare himself, and wait."

Then, at last the "call" really came. This was on the occasion of Jesus' baptism at the hand of John the Baptist in the Jordan (SPP-75). For the Evangelists this event was "the effective beginning of his ministry, the moment of his designation as king of Israel" (SPP-74). For God it was the occasion on which he acknowledged Jesus as "his messianic son and representative" (SPP-74). For Schonfield it was a genuine "experience" that must be acknowledged as occurring in Jesus' spiritual life, a fulfillment of what he had hoped and believed would occur (SPP-75). "Tradition," Schonfield suggests, is responsible for the ideas that at the time Jesus heard a voice from heaven and saw the Spirit descending upon him as a dove (SPP-75). But whatever the source of the Gospel narrative as it has come down to us, our author believes we must credit it with giving "appositely and graphically" an account of the "experience" that in reality was Jesus' own.

I have not been able to find a passage in Schonfield's book in which he specifically employs the term "Messiah secret." But that he believes that there was such—in the sense of Schweitzer rather than in that of Wrede—is clear. Thus, he remarks that as Jesus' fame spread abroad, the Pharisees were at times puzzled, at times furious, because of his undoubted claim to an authority for which they could find no justification in such a one as he appeared to be. They, therefore, took him for "a religious upstart and demagogue," and they attributed his popular appeal to the

working of "the prince of the demons" through him
(SPP-77). But had Jesus let it be known that he was
God's Messiah in the early days of his ministry, the result
would have been nothing less than "disastrous," for the
Romans would have interpreted such a confession as
"treasonable sedition" (SPP-80). Hence, Jesus' speaking
to the common people in parables lest "spies and inform-
ers" should tell the authorities of his "highly political as
well as spiritual theme of the Kingdom of God" (SPP-
81). Hence also, Jesus' use of the enigmatic term "Son
of Man (i.e., the Man)" to refer to himself, for to com-
paratively few would this mean the Messiah (SPP-82).
Hence finally, his choice of strong physical specimens such
as the two pairs of fisherman brothers as his "bodyguard"
(SPP-83). And it is to be recalled, too, that with such, he
could readily flee across the lake to the Decapolis, the ter-
ritory of the ten Greek cities, where they would all be safe
(SPP-83).

Jesus' ministry and teaching had both its successes and
its failures. These latter moved him deeply and brought
forth anger from him (SPP-86 f.), though at the same
time he probably anticipated from Isa. 6:9-10 that he
would be rejected by his people, as the "Teacher of Righteousness" had been. In any event, the death of John the
Baptist at the hand of Antipas was a warning of the grave
danger with which he was surrounded. Accordingly, Jesus
now realized that the disclosure of his Messiahship must at
once be made to his disciples. This came to realization in
the Caesarea Philippi experience through Jesus' drawing
out of Peter's confession and his own approval of the same
(SPP-92).

This event inaugurated the "second phase of his ministry," one in which Jesus for the first time spoke of his approaching sufferings and death (SPP-92). No doubt,

Schonfield holds, the early Christian writers went beyond Jesus' own words in bringing his passion narrative into conformity with "the Oracles" to be gleaned from Psalms and Prophets (SPP-95-97). But Jesus, as well as the later church, had read all these and pondered deeply on them and their relation to the Messiah, and he had through them been enabled to transcend the "vagueness of contemporary Messianism" and to bring the picture of the Messiah into "singular focus" (SPP-94). So we have no right "to jettison the whole story" as told by the Evangelists at this point, particularly in view of the fact that these writers at times themselves "did not realise the worth or importance" of what they recorded! (SPP-97).

Now, indeed, Jesus has to look forward to what is to prove both "difficult and dangerous," a task that will require of him "utmost caution" and both "careful organisation and timing" (SPP-99). The task is to be threefold, viz.: (a) "to deliver his prophetic call to national repentance" at the capital (i.e., Jerusalem); (b) to show himself to the "Jewish authorities" there; and (c) "to set the stage" for his revealing himself for what he has long held he was, the Messiah (SPP-106). With all this in view, Jesus steadfastly "set his face to go to Jerusalem" (Luke 9:51), established a base of operations at the home of Lazarus in Bethany, and chose a young priest (John?) to make "contact with secret disciples and sympathisers in the Sanhedrin" (SPP-109-111).

The so-called raising of Lazarus, "who made a surprising recovery after being apparently dead" was for the Sanhedrin "the last straw" (SPP-116). Their presiding chairman, the high priest Caiaphas, had said, "It is expedient for you that one man should die for the people" (John 11:50), that is, there was grave danger that a popular movement led by Jesus might bring the wrath of Rome down upon the nation. Accordingly, it was decided that "Jesus would have to be liquidated" (SPP-117).

But Jesus soon got word of this through Nicodemus, his friend within the circle of the authorities, and began to make his own preparations for Passion Week. These gradually came to fruition after this fashion:

a. He had arranged, possibly through Lazarus, for the foal of an ass to be tied at the entrance to Bethany village and had given those concerned a couple of passwords to exchange with the disciples whom he should send for the animal. In terms of Zech. 9:9, Jesus would enter Jerusalem. The disciples soon grasped the implications of this arrangement and welcomed him as true Messiah in fulfillment of the prophecy (SPP-119).

b. The cleansing of the Temple came next. This represented a neat challenge of the chief priests' "vested interest" in what was going on at the stalls; for they well knew that often the poor were charged exorbitant prices for what was required for the Temple sacrifices. The "duel of wits" that followed between Jesus and themselves put them on the horns of the dilemma relative to John's prophetic stature, and Jesus clearly won this round with the populace (SPP-124).

c. The question regarding the paying of the poll tax due in A.D. 34-35 was dealt with by Jesus with the same assurance that he displayed in other matters. His auditors knew that Jesus meant "God is our sole Lord"; so all Caesar could expect from any Jew would be "his miserable silver." The "subtle contempt" displayed in Jesus' answer toward the sycophants of Rome to be found among the Jewish authorities was not lost upon his audience (SPP-126).

d. Though it is not always easy to follow the course of

events throughout this last week, Schonfield, like Schweitzer, believes that the necessity which Jesus felt of making the true history conform to the blueprint to be found in Scripture may well serve us as guide. Jesus was "obsessed" with the need of making the one history conform to the other (SPP-132). This was, as Schweitzer had observed, the fantastic world of apocalypticism—it suited and evidenced either a "sick mind," or a "genius" (SPP-133). Thus, Jesus even prepared for the fulfillment of Ps. 41:9 through inducing Mary to anoint him with the costly nard. This was to trigger Judas' "cupidity" that Jesus might be betrayed by him and so fulfill the oracle (SPP-135 f.).

e. Next comes the Last Supper in the upper room. On this occasion also, Jesus had made all the arrangements; the young man with the waterpot—an exceptional sight in the Orient, where it is the women who draw water—would lead the disciples to the place Jesus had prepared, thus revealing his "generalship" (SPP-138 f.).

f. The trials come next. Schonfield, like some other modern scholars, is inclined to blame the later church through its Gospels for stressing "the guilt of the Jews" and attempting to "whitewash Pilate" (SPP-129). Actually, the meeting of the Sanhedrin was, "not to try Jesus," but to arrive at the means of formulating an "indictment" of him that might be laid before the governor with a view to his "summary execution" (SPP-147). Jesus' theology was never in question, therefore, before the Sanhedrin, merely rather "his political pretensions." In relating the hearings of Jesus before the authorities—Jewish and Roman—Schonfield generally follows the account in John, ch. 18 and 19. On the whole, he accepts the image of Pilate portrayed in the Gospels and believes that Pilate finally gave in to the Jewish appeal when they cried out, "If you release this man, you are not Caesar's friend" (John 19:12). (SPP-147-154.)

g. In connection with the crucifixion, Schonfield's most significant statements for his views relative to Jesus' scheming methods have to do with the nature of the liquid which the Gospels say he drank. Schonfield has no doubt that this was "a drug" administered by someone whom Joseph of Arimathea, in accord with Jesus' wishes, had arranged to be present for the purpose and to await Jesus' signal with the words, "I am thirsty." (SPP-165-167.) At once, Jesus' "body sagged" as the drug took effect and he appeared like "a dead man." However, at this point the Roman soldier, going his rounds to see whether the criminals were dead, spoiled Jesus' well-laid plans by spearing him in the side (SPP-168), a thrust that no doubt actually brought on his death, and so Jesus, while he perhaps revived temporarily after being brought out of the tomb where he had been placed, soon died and had to be reinterred in a convenient spot (SPP-172). Schonfield then endeavors to account for the empty tomb in as rational a fashion as possible.

h. As for the resurrection appearances, Schonfield makes shift with these in a variety of ways. He sets forth as vital his belief that the church is undoubtedly right in saying that such a great spiritual movement could not have been founded on a "deliberate falsehood" to the effect that Jesus "had risen from the dead" (SPP-170 f.). The visions of the disciples were "not subjective"; they did see "*a real living person*" (SPP-173). The problem is simply— who was this person? Perhaps in the case of the women, it was the "gardener" (SPP-174), who then became "an angel" and later still "two angels." Possibly it was the man who had administered the drug to Jesus (SPP-175). Other appearances in Judea are questionable, as are also those in Galilee (SPP-175-179). On the whole, Schonfield inclines to the view that it was the same young man all along in all the appearances. He was the one whom Jesus had arranged with about the drug and who had loyally endeavored to carry out Jesus' dying wish also that he should speak to Peter and the others of a rendezvous in Galilee. Schonfield does not claim that "this is the solution" of the problem (SPP-179). But from the Jewish viewpoint that a man's messenger (his angel, or his *shaliach*) is "as himself," it goes some way to account for the identification of Master and his accredited representative following the death of the former (SPP-180).

CRITIQUE

Of the five "Jewish" interpretations of Jesus of Nazareth discussed in this book, this writer feels peculiarly drawn to this of Schonfield. His frank acceptance of the idea that we may, indeed, know the mind of the historic Jesus relative to himself is, this writer finds, refreshing. He does not make Jesus out as creative as C. H. Dodd finds him to be (DAS-110), and as this writer could wish, but as indicated above he refuses to "jettison" the Gospel account as a whole when it declares Jesus to be set upon fulfilling the Messianic prophecies. In this determination, Schonfield finds solid contact with the true Jesus (SPP-14), and in working out the details of his *Plot,* consciously or unconsciously, he is following Schweitzer in attributing the "dogmatic history" that overlies the "true history" in the Gospels to Jesus' mind and not to that of the Evangelists.

In *The Intention of Jesus*—to be glanced at in Chapter 7, below, along with others of the last three decades—this

writer had occasion to draw upon much of the same data
as that examined by Schonfield, and both writers owe
much to the work of Schweitzer, particularly to his examination of the events of Passion Week. The very similarity
of the titles of the two books—*The Intention of Jesus* and
The Passover Plot—is suggestive. Up to a point they agree
in their deductions, as in both cases they are impelled to
look to Jesus for the source of the motivation they find in
the Gospel story. To state the same thought in other
terms, *they agree relative to the "Messiah secret" that its
author was Jesus and not the church.*

To tabulate, then, a few of the points in which the writer
would agree with Schonfield—the list is not intended
to be exhaustive, but it would include these items: (*a*)
Jesus found himself laid under the necessity of awaiting
his "call," even as the prophets before him had done, before he could act; (*b*) this "call" came to him on the
banks of the Jordan, its outward manifestation being
found in his "anointing" at the Baptist's hands; (*c*) Jesus'
temptations were real and his decisions with reference to
them played a large part in the course his ministry was to
take; (*d*) that ministry had its ups and downs, its successes and failures when these are viewed from the standpoint of Jesus' motivation as this is factually narrated in
the Gospels; (*e*) Jesus well knew his own mind relative to
the sort of Messiah God wished him to be and he set out
from the beginning of his activity to achieve that high calling; and finally, (*f*) with the coming of Passion Week,
when the fruition of all his activities came into focus,
Jesus was prepared to take matters wholly into his own
hands and to direct the course of events to the accomplish-
ment of his goal. It is at just this point—having come so
far with Schonfield—that for over two decades the present
writer has found it necessary to part company with the

type of conclusion to which Schonfield's logic takes him. This, as will be shown in Chapter 7, is to be expected, one imagines, as they belong fundamentally to different religious cultures.

And now, as we look back over Schonfield's thesis with a view to criticism of certain points in its minutiae, the writer feels impelled to remark that it is just in these matters of diversity between the Jewish tradition, on the one hand, and the Christian, on the other, that their differences are found to lie and, indeed, must lie if the two traditions are not to merge and become one in this problem of the mind of Jesus of Nazareth! Let us discuss here but a few particular items of this character, items that are almost, if not quite, peculiar to Schonfield's presentation of his case.

1. Schonfield sees a sort of "blueprint" for the Messiah to follow in the prophetic writings, and if this writer understands him correctly, Schonfield feels that Jesus had already found this and determined to accept it for his own ministry. Shortly after the appearance of *The Intention of Jesus* (1943), the late Clarence Craig took the writer to task as holding just this view of Jesus' thought about his ministry, that is, as he expressed it, of finding out "from a book" what God desired him to do.

The reply in the *Journal of Religion,* January, 1945, page 58, was that this writer had nowhere "suggested that Jesus discovered from a book what his career would be like." Rather, "Jesus knew that the cross awaited him because his intimate communion with his Father had made their minds and wills one, because he had from the very first no illusions about the sinfulness of human nature, because he knew the tragedies which had characterized the experiences of prophets before him. That he found in the Scriptures of those same prophets three great figures—the

Messiah, the Son of Man, the Suffering Servant—which, combined, would answer to his creative purpose was simply because he had made those Scriptures his spiritual food from his youth upward."

The present writer would add also, what indeed he has written elsewhere, that essentially Jesus knew he was what we have just remarked *because he knew himself,* he knew himself to be these things. This places him at the pinnacle of the Hebrew prophetic line, and one may ask, *Is it not strange that, when it is a known characteristic of this line that its members severally knew the tasks committed to them by God at their "call," the head of the line should be challenged as not knowing what his task was?* Or, alternatively, that the church in its Scriptures should show itself so morally blind as to misrepresent his mind about himself? At this point, then, Schonfield and this writer are nearer together than either is to those others of whom we have spoken, possibly even nearer than the writer has understood us to be! May this be so.

2. This writer must break a lance with Schonfield relative to what has been called the *overtone* that is found throughout his book, that is, that the alternatives before Christianity at the start were limited to what might be termed "Jewish" or "Pagan." *Here is a third,* viz., the continuing guidance of the Spirit of the Living God, that same Spirit that had inspired the Hebrew prophetic line and that one might suggest was still to be found at work on the contemporary scene, particularly among the *Ḥasidim,* the "saintly," the "poor," the "meek"—in other words, among the nonsectaries, certainly, a large bulk of the current Jewish people. This group was in no sense "organised" nor did it produce a literature. We are not, therefore, in a position to trace Jesus' thought to it; it was composed of the sort of decent, upright folk that to a degree have formed the core

of the society built up round the Biblical revelation and pursuing the Biblical "way of life" from time immemorial. Many Biblical scholars have thought that no doubt the "holy family" perhaps of Jesus' disciples, particularly those from Galilee, emerged from among these nonsectaries of whom we are speaking. (See frontispiece.)

Jesus, himself, if as this writer conceives him to have belonged to these *Hasidim* of his day, would quite likely not have thought it essential to have given birth to a new body of literature. Rather, the most important single factor in his teaching would have been the bypassing of all contemporary solidified forms of Judaism in order to return to the spirit and teachings of the prophets before him, not, however, to rest there in a state of religious and moral stagnation, but with a view to securing a firm footing for the new start which the Spirit of his Father was prompting him to make. His aim, as not alone the passage at Matt. 5:17 distinctly states, was, *not* "to abolish the law and the prophets," but rather "to *implement* them," that is, to indicate another method for putting them into operation than the one prescribed by "scribes and Pharisees" (v. 20). The latter was one of adding thousands of statutes in order to apply the Scriptures to life situations (as later found in Mishnah and Talmud), while his was through the acquisition of a new spirit, a right attitude, a godlike motivation.

This dramatic return to the spirit of the Hebrew prophets on Jesus' part is in my judgment as certain an event as any associated in the Gospel narratives with his career. It is the moral equivalent of the Reformation which in the sixteenth century endeavored to bypass the catholicism of the intervening centuries and return to the simplicity of first-century Christianity. Obviously, it rejects Schonfield's "either-or" in terms of the current Judaism versus Paganism. It even goes so far as to raise the further question whether the Christian faith is not far nearer in spirit to that put forth by the Hebrew prophets long ages before, nearer in discernment of the true nature of God, nearer in true respect for man the individual and love for man the universal.

3. As for the course of events during Passion Week and Jesus' dominant relation to them, one is inclined to agree with Schonfield for the most part, as this writer has written elsewhere at some length. He finds, for example, no quarrel with Schonfield's arguing for Jesus' part in setting the stage for the so-called triumphal entry and the scene of the Last Supper in the upper room, nor for the essential meaning which he attaches to the incident of the *"denarius,"* nor would one be concerned to argue over whether Jesus' appearances before the Sanhedrin were in the nature of a trial or merely of a meeting to draw up an "indictment." This, as Schonfield shows, in no way relieves the Sanhedrin of a certain responsibility for what transpired regardless of the later church's endeavor to heighten the guilt of the Jewish authorities in the matter. If this writer may express his own judgment at this point —it has always appeared relatively inconsequential who in the first instance was responsible for crucifying Jesus; the problem today is lest by word or thought or action one crucify him afresh for oneself (Heb. 6:6).

The nub of Schonfield's argument, however, concerns the matter of the "drug" which he thinks was, through Jesus' own connivance, administered to him at the last. There is no adequate evidence of this, however; quite the contrary—the Synoptic evidence is clear that Jesus was twice offered something to drink while on the cross, or so it is in the accounts of Mark and Matthew (Mark 15:23, 36; Matt. 27:34, 48), Luke independently, it would seem, relating the matter as a single act (Luke 23:36). In all

three Evangelists what Jesus accepted was the mere sour
wine or vinegar of the Roman soldiery; and in the accounts of Mark and Matthew, wherein he was presented at
the *beginning* of the incident with wine mingled with
"gall" (Matt.) or "myrrh" (Mark) for their soporific
effect, *both Evangelists are careful to state that he would
not accept this mixture.* So that in stating that Jesus was
administered a "drug" which stupefied him and gave the
appearance of death, Schonfield is relying solely on the
evidence of certain manuscripts and versions of the one
verse of John 19:29. Here, too, the great majority of
convincing witnesses (Greek, Latin, and Coptic) read as
do the Synoptics. There is probably but a single line of
testimony (generally called "Caesarean"), whose origin is
much disputed, that inserts "myrrh" as having been contained in the vinegar offered to Jesus at the end. And this
anomaly (sour wine mingled with bitter myrrh!) probably
represents a careless scribal combining of all the Evangelists' (including John's) "sour wine" which came at the
end of the experience with Mark's "myrrh" taken from the
beginning (Mark 15:23).

Schonfield's entire argument, therefore, based on the
idea that Jesus had been merely drugged on the cross, to
the effect that he had intended to simulate death and following resurrection, is seen to be based on the slenderest
possible evidence.

In accepting Schonfield's argument (or, this writer
might even say, having foreseen it some twenty-five years
earlier than his book!), relative to Jesus' masterly "generalship" as he went about his ministry, determining a la
Schweitzer the course the history was to take, this writer
did so because he felt that the golden thread running
through Jesus' work and ministry was to be seen in the cas-
ual hint of a word spoken here, an action taken there (oft-

times without the Evangelist's own understanding of its relevance, SPP-97; PCB-736). This principle could be applied to many of his pre-Passion Week activities but particularly to the manner in which during that week he challenged every Jewish group to accept him for what he knew himself to be. But, *in all this activity there was no single breath of deception or trickery on Jesus' part.* One cannot say as much, however hard one may try, of the sort of expedient that would be involved in deliberately accepting a draft of wine mingled with myrrh for its soporific effect!

4. This writer's own final comment on Schonfield's contribution to the field of inquiry relates to his speaking (as many do) of Jesus as the *Jewish* Messiah. However gracious this may be (and is, indeed), it does not give expression to the depth of the Hebrew prophetic insight, which, as we shall see in Chapter 7, foresaw the Messiah of the "remnant" and, therefore, *of no group conceived on national lines*, but rather of *all mankind in their individual commitment* (a la Bultmann).

5

The "Para-Zealot" Revolutionary

This book had to be written!

The book in question is S. G. F. Brandon's *Jesus and the Zealots* (1967). Note the date; by then, Jesus had been assigned a place in one or other of all the sects and groups of the contemporary Judaism with the exception of the Sadducees and Zealots. The Sadducees were out as Jesus was not an Aaronic priest. So only the Zealots remained for some historian to discover evidence that Jesus had belonged to this party or its like.

Then, too, since Nazi days and even more since Yigael Yadin's remarkable finds at Masada, renewed interest in and sympathy for the Zealots as the one organized "resistance" movement against the might of Rome have been manifest (BJZ-24, Chs. 4, 7). That Jewish Christianity, then, should have represented a sort of "para-Zealot movement" (BJZ-201) is a thesis presenting exciting possibilities for research on the part of the historian who is interested only in "acute and careful interrogation of the evidence" and not in a "facile" or "sensational" solution to the problem involved (BJZ-xiv)!

There is yet another reason for this book's being written. For it proves to be the *reductio ad absurdum* of the *Sitz im Leben* motif introduced into Biblical studies by Rudolf

Bultmann. Brandon says quite frankly that the Gospel account of Jesus' trial and crucifixion when studied in the light of the needs of the "Christian community" at the time proves not to be an "objective historical record." It is shown rather to be the product of "apologetical factors" relating to the community's life situation (BJZ-xiv).

We make much of this last item merely because our author does himself. Examination of the motive(s) involved in the writing of the Gospels is basic to Brandon's entire argument and takes up much space in his book. The *Sitz im Leben* tool functions as follows:

a. The historian first learns all that is possible relating to the *life situation* of the ancient writer he is studying and/or that of his hypothetical readers;

b. This life situation will suggest the obvious *motive* of the ancient writer in composing his book;

c. This motive will have appeared to the ancient writer to justify any *retouching of either historical narrative or character* with which the writer is dealing, with a view to solving some problem in the contemporary life situation of his readers;

d. The *product of this process* is the ancient writer's composition now in the historian's hands; accordingly,

e. The historian may now proceed to examine it with the *objectivity* which is his constant aim in dealing with the history of the ancient past.

Employing this tool and approaching every historical problem with the sense of objective perspective it calls for, the modern historian has succeeded in "debunking" much that has passed for history in bygone ages. Toward the close of the present chapter we propose to bring to our readers' notice a striking example of the use of this tool in reverse, so to speak. Meanwhile, we proceed to an examination of Brandon's use of it.

Professor Brandon's Argument

The question to which Brandon addresses his historical investigation is one that cannot be avoided since it is well attested, indeed, "the most certain thing known about Jesus" (BJZ-1), this, namely, "Why did the Roman governor of Judaea decide to execute Jesus for sedition?" (BJZ-xiii). This question may and probably will give many Christians offense, for the reason that they cannot conceive of Jesus having any "political views" (BJZ-24). Yet, if he did not, why did he choose a Zealot (or, as I believe, two such) for a disciple? Why, moreover, was he crucified between two "brigands" (probably "Jewish resistance fighters") (BJZ-xiv)? What did he mean when he said, "I came not to bring peace, but a sword" (Matt. 10:34; BJZ-vi)? And again on the brink of his capture in Gethsemane when he checked over his disciples' "armament" (Luke 22:35-38; BJZ-340n7), what was his motivation if not political in flavor? Such in essentials is the historical problem.

Now, we come to the *Sitz im Leben,* the situation in life, with which it is concerned. And at once, according to the historian Brandon, we run into difficulties. For, when we turn to the contemporary Christian accounts we find them apparently trying to give us a rereading of the incident of the trial and death of Jesus that will present them as "a tragic miscarriage of justice," one indeed for which, not Pilate, but "the Jews were essentially responsible" (BJZ-5). Mark, too, makes Pilate out "a fool beyond belief" in presenting to the Jews "a choice between Jesus and Barabbas"—this could only have been "the act of an idiot" (BJZ-4). This strange attitude of Mark toward the closing events of Jesus' life, shown as well by other like

examples (BJZ-6-10), suggests that he is endeavoring to
cover up the true facts about Jesus' attitude toward Rome
(BJZ-10).

So we turn to other original sources to discover what
these facts are, or, at least, we endeavor to do so. But
these are not readily discovered. Paul is our most obvious
contemporary witness; his writings antedate Mark's Gospel by ten years or more (BJZ-10 ff.). But unfortunately, Paul's "conception of Jesus" and the historical
Jesus of Nazareth have little in common. Paul's view of
Jesus is "transcendental" in the extreme and geared in
with an "esoteric soteriology" that has no parallel in the
"Jewish thought" of the times (BJZ-12). So no help can
be had from Paul on the subject of Jesus' true motivations.

We may turn, then, to the oldest Jewish Christian community—that of the church in Jerusalem. The *Sitz im
Leben* of this Christian group would perhaps be nearest to
that of Jesus, could we but discover what it was like. Unfortunately, however, this ancient church ceased to exist
with the fall of Jerusalem in A.D. 70 and all its records per-
ished with it. The legendary account of its members having fled to Pella across the Jordan on this occasion cannot
be credited. In any case, the destruction of all record of it
leaves open the question as to whether this old church itself may have "made common cause with their country-
men" against Rome (BJZ-15).

Further evidence of Jesus' motivation is scanty in the
extreme. There are a few scattered bits of testimony in the
other Gospels (Matthew, Luke, and John); these will
have to be examined in due course (BJZ-15-18). What we
are able to conclude may be summed up thus: both before
and after Jesus' death and resurrection, his disciples believed him to be the Messiah "who would 'restore the

kingdom to Israel' " (BJZ-18), and his enemies (the Jewish and Roman authorities) both came to think him "a
dangerous Messianic pretender" (BJZ-20). But we must
still remain in doubt as to what he thought of himself
(BJZ-20 f.). And it is this doubt, together with the hints
already mentioned, that raise the problem for us of Jesus'
possible relation to the Zealots' nationalistic aspirations
(BJZ-21).

Stultified as we have just seen in his endeavor to discover from the New Testament the true *Sitz im Leben*
both of the historical Jesus and of the early church which
has transmitted to us the image of its Master, Brandon
turns to such other contemporary records as are available.
This "switch" causes him to write two long and most informative chapters in which he presents a useful summary
of what is known about "The Zealots: Their Origin and
Ideals" (BJZ-26-64) and "Israel's Cause Against Rome,
A.D. 6-73" (BJZ-65-145). These two chapters need only
to be perused for the student to discover the large amount
of painstaking research that has gone into their composition. They are refreshingly interesting and characterized
by a wealth of creative suggestions for further research.

For our purposes the most important cluster of ideas
that emerge from these chapters may be suggested by a
quotation or two in Brandon's own words. These are—the
thought basic to Yahwism on which all Jewish nationalism
has based its claims, "that Yahweh had chosen the nation
to be his own peculiar people and had given to them the
land of Canaan as their home and peculiar possession
(BJZ-62); and the complementary thought that every Jew
who loved his homeland would have seen an "insult" in
the presence of the power of Rome in the Holy Land
(BJZ-63). Hence, as Brandon insists, "Zealotism" is to be

seen as a proper and normative addendum to the faith of
the fathers professed by every contemporary Jew. It is not
surprising, then, that modern Israel has made of Masada
"a national monument" (BJZ-64; see further App. 4).

In the second of the chapters above mentioned, Brandon traces the progress of the Zealot movement during the
period of Jesus' life from boyhood to the crucifixion. He
stresses among other things its normative character (BJZ-
68), the evidence from the Gospels of their writers'
knowledge of the troubled state of affairs at the time ("the
insurrection," Mark 15:7; the two thieves crucified with
Jesus, Mark 15:27; the slaughter of the Galileans referred
to in Luke 13:1-3; Jesus' reference to the violent men at
Matt. 11:12, and the like; BJZ-78), and the evidence for
crucifixion being suffered by many Zealots (BJZ-103 f.,
145). Brandon even goes so far as to suggest that a cross
symbolized Zealot martyrdom before its adoption as a
Christian sign (BJZ-145), and that Jesus' reference to
cross-bearing (Mark 8:34) may have been taken over
from the Zealots (BJZ-57, 145)! He has also a lengthy
discussion of Josephus' well-known section on the stoning
of "James, the brother of Jesus, 'the so-called Christ' "
(BJZ-115-127), and from this he concludes that the
church in Jerusalem just previous to the First Jewish War
(A.D. 63-73) was far more attached to the aspirations of
the lower classes of the priesthood and to the Zealot
cause than to the aristocracy among the former
(BJZ-125 f.). Our author concludes this section of his
book with the claim that the Zealots were genuine successors of the Old Testament prophets and that they believed
that Israel had been foreseen by the prophets to be the
"Elect People of Yahweh" (BJZ-145).

Such, then, was the life situation of the Palestine in
which Jesus grew up and in which for its short lifetime

Jewish Christianity flourished. It was characterized by extreme "tension" and held in it elements of "hatred," "fear," and the certainty of the near approach of the end of the age (BJZ-147). The church's recollection of what Jesus was and said is bound to have been colored by the early community and its reaction to this dire situation. Its "memory" would be an "amalgam" of the two primary elements (situation plus what Jesus actually was) and this would certainly take on a certain coloring from the church's demands for solutions to its problems (BJZ-148).

Accordingly, we are now at points c through e of the *Sitz im Leben* technique as found above. This constitutes the rest of Brandon's book (Chs. 4 to 7). Brandon's first concern now is to discover how the early Jewish Church reacted to the current situation, hoping that we may thereafter take the second step of finding out what Jesus' reaction to that situation was, and then, of course, his major concern(s) and aim(s).

JEWISH CHRISTIANITY IN THIS SITUATION

The first of these concerns is examined by our author in his chapter entitled "The Jewish Christians and the Zealot Ideal" (BJZ-146-220). With a wealth of erudition and following the pattern of much of scholarly method since the days of F. C. Bauer (1835), Brandon concludes that these earliest Christians were eminently loyal to the faith of their fathers, being true Jews and seeing Jesus' ministry as strictly confined to his own people (BJZ-174). Moreover, they were firm in their belief in the divine election of Israel through Abraham (BJZ-171). For these Jewish followers of Jesus, he was the Jewish Messiah, and their sin-

gle problem relating to his efforts concerned the fact that
he had not succeeded in restoring the kingdom to Israel
(BJZ-175-182; see Acts 1:6). Rather he had died "a
martyr to Roman hate and Jewish blindness" (BJZ-182).
In this Jewish gospel, there was no room for the Gentiles.
Instead, Israel's victory at the hand of Yahweh implied
Rome's sure defeat and punishment for the *Goyim* (Gentiles) (BJZ-182). This had not yet happened, but the day
was not far away when, with the Messiah's return, it would
occur. For God had raised him up and the Jewish Church
awaited with eagerness his coming again to complete his
unfinished task (BJZ-190). Brandon admits that this re-
construction is based on evidence that is "indirect, circum-
stantial, and problematic" in some part (BJZ-189), yet it
is "consistent and intelligible" in its results.

All in all, our author finds it possible to conclude that
Jewish Christianity had much in common with "zealots in
sympathy and purpose; indeed some of their adherents
were probably also professed adherents of Zealotism"
(BJZ-219). This attitude should reflect that of their Master himself, Brandon believes. Hence the next step in the
argument is to discover whether this is so, and if not, for
example in the N.T.'s "key document" (Mark's Gospel),
why not? It is with a view to examining this question,
then, that our author addresses himself to the subject of
Ch. 5, "The Markan Gospel: An *Apologia ad Christianos
Romanos.*"

Brandon begins his argument at this point with a statement of the view (held by many N.T. scholars) that
Mark's Gospel is to be associated with Rome, as both
church tradition and the Latinisms in the Gospel would
suggest (BJZ-221). These are "weighty reasons," he
believes, and to these he adds the suggestion that probably

the Gospels all emanated from large centers of the faith, Mark particularly, short and seemingly relatively unimportant as it is, requiring some such backing to have resulted in its preservation (BJZ-222).

The date of this Gospel is something else again and not so easily determined. Our author settles on the period immediately following the destruction of Jerusalem in A.D. 70 and the giving of the "Flavian triumph in Rome" the following year (BJZ-222-242). He arrives at this date as this Gospel's *Sitz im Leben* by reason of the stress found in it on the following events: first, Jesus' endorsement of paying tribute to Caesar (Mark 12:17), a motif that Brandon does not believe Mark portrays correctly, though his interest in the matter helps us to observe an element in the life situation in which he writes and this fits only into the Roman *locus* "shortly after A.D. 71" (BJZ-224-227, 270-271, 345-349); secondly, Mark's concern about the rending of the veil of the Temple (Mark 15:38) at Jesus' death is aroused by the fact that "the purple curtains of the Temple" had been carried in the Triumph referred to above and so would be present to the minds of the Roman people in this year (BJZ-227-229); thirdly, Mark, ch. 13, with its "Abomination of Desolation" (v. 14) and its general description of the profanation of the Temple and final destruction of Jerusalem clearly has reference to the events of A.D. 70 (Titus' entering of the Most Holy Place and the erection of the Roman standards in the Temple area together with the legion's sacrificing to them, BJZ-230-233); fourthly, add to this description the prophecy with reference to the Parousia which Mark says Jesus went out of his way to make on this occasion (Mark 13:1-3), though at his trial Mark appears to deny any such reference to destruction of the Temple by Jesus or to

his return (BJZ-233-236)—at the least such stress in
Mark's Gospel shows that the recent events connected
with the Temple were "in the news" at Rome.

All this evidence serves to connect Mark with Rome at
a particular date. But we may go farther than this and see
that Mark had in view the necessity, at this place and date,
of presenting a brief on behalf of the Jewish Christian
community in Rome, an *apologia,* or defense, indeed, that
would serve to dissociate the Christian faith and its constituency from the rest of the Judaism of the day so far as
the thinking of the Roman authorities was concerned. This
necessity lay in the presence at Rome of widespread
"anti-Semitism," or as Josephus termed it "hatred of the
Jews" (BJZ-226 and n3). Mark's endeavor to draw away
such hatred from the Christian part of the Jewish community is seen in several passages; for example, in his relating Isa. 46:7 with Jer. 7:11 and placing both in the mouth
of Jesus on the occasion of the cleansing of the Temple
(Mark 11:17; BJZ-237). Mark wished in this way to attribute to Jesus the desire that "non-Jewish peoples"
should be welcomed into the Temple. His embarrassment,
too, at the fact that one of Jesus' disciples (Simon) was a
Zealot, was concealed by using the Aramaic equivalent
(*Qanana,* Greek *Kananaios*) for this designation so hate-
ful to all Romans (BJZ-243-245). Then, too, Mark's
quite evident endeavor to shift the guilt of the Roman execution of Jesus by crucifixion from them to the shoulders
of the Jewish authorities has not only "set the pattern for
the other Gospels," but "for all subsequent Christian
thinking" as well (BJZ-245-264).

But Brandon is not yet done with Mark. This Evangelist's "anti-Jewish thesis" (BJZ-279) is found to necessi-
tate his demonstrating two further points for which he
provides the requisite proof: viz. (*a*) that the Jewish peo-

ple by and large did not approve of Jesus' aims and so at
last sought his death (BJZ-265-273) and (*b*) that Jesus
did not awaken faith in these aims even among his own
friends and family (BJZ-274-280).

The upshot of this entire investigation, and it is detailed
and documented to the last minutia of detail, is Brandon's
firm conviction that Jesus was put to death as a "rebel"
against the Roman regime, not as one who had ever abandoned his Jewish faith (BJZ-282). We are able, our author believes, to see through Mark's thinly veiled
anti-Jewish motivation and to piece together the actual
historic events approximately as they occurred. For it is
the discovery of the actual *Sitz im Leben* of the Jewish
Christian community in Rome just after the Flavian triumph in A.D. 71 that makes clear just how Mark was provided with his motive for writing such an *Apologia* as we
find in his Gospel.

The other three Evangelists had a variety of other motives for writing their Gospels, all related in some part to
but not entirely to be identified with Mark's. It is these
which form the topic of interest in Brandon's next chapter
entitled "The Concept of the Pacific Christ: Its Origin and
Development."

Briefly, these motives—all arising out of the life situations in which they originate—are as follows: first, Matthew ("the most Jewish of the Gospels") probably should
be located in Alexandria, the city containing the largest
number of Jews in the Empire, and some ten or fifteen
years later than Mark (BJZ-284, 290). This time and
place are important because some of the *Sicarii* escaping
from Jerusalem after its fall in A.D. 70 had been rounded
up in Alexandria by the Jews and handed over to their
Roman masters (BJZ-291); there may even have been
some of the survivors of the Jerusalem Church who simi-

larly reached Alexandria (BJZ-294). These latter and
their Christian compatriots already in Alexandria would
probably view the destruction of Jerusalem and the
disastrous outcome of the First Jewish War as Yahweh's
punishment of "Israel for its rejection of Jesus" (BJZ-
293), and this view would surely motivate a Gospel written in Alexandria at the time (BJZ-300).

That Matthew exhibits such motivation appears to be
clear, as mention of some of this Gospel's exclusive features suggests. These are Matthew's sole relating of the
flight of the holy family into Egypt (Matt. 2:13), now
paralleled by a similar fleeing on the part of Jewish Christians from "the furious Heathen" (the Romans, BJZ-
297); Peter's exaltation in Matt. 16:17-19 to the position
of "primus" in the apostolic band, an event of great interest, to say the least, in the largest Jewish city outside Palestine (a daughter colony of the "Mother Church" and its
Christian constituency, BJZ-299) and one that would
serve to place Peter up as Paul's chief competitor, a matter of no little importance in view of Paul's low estimate of
the church in Alexandria (BJZ-302; see also 197 f.);
Matthew's introduction of Pilate's wife to speak in Jesus'
behalf (Matt. 27:19), Pilate's own disavowal of guilt in
sentencing Jesus by the washing of his hands (v. 24), and
the Jewish people's assuming this responsibility on their
own (v. 25)—a denouement "intended to have a chas-
tening significance for his readers in Alexandria" (BJZ-
304); and the additions to the parable of the wicked hus-
bandmen in Matthew which underline the idea of Jerusalem's plight being an act of "divine retribution" (Matt.
21:33-46; BJZ-304).

The end result of the Evangelist's so viewing the implication of *the whole Jewish people* in the death of Jesus is
his determination to paint the portrait of the "pacific

Christ" who would have nothing of fighting and war, even of self-defense, but was rather a messenger of peace. This appears from Matthew's account of the Gethsemane episode (Matt. 26:52-54), the nature of Jesus' teaching in the Beatitudes, his experience of temptation, and his lament over Jerusalem (BJZ-306-315).

Secondly, Luke who wrote his Gospel and The Acts "some fifteen or twenty years after Mark" and for Achaia (BJZ-286, 315 f.), too, had his reasons for emphasizing "the pacific character of Jesus." His endeavor was to show the faith acceptable to Gentiles and protected by the magistrates of Rome (BJZ-316). He does this more subtly than Matthew, but he does it nonetheless. Witness the angel's song (Luke 2:14), the parables of the good Samaritan and the prodigal son, Jesus' dealing summarily with his disciples who would call down the fire of heaven on a group of Samaritans (ch. 9:52-56), and his references to the retribution that befell some at the fall of the tower at Siloam and Pilate's slaughtering the Galileans (ch. 13:1-5). Numerous additions of Luke to the story of the trials and crucifixion of Jesus tell the same story (BJZ-317 f.).

Lastly, in the Fourth Gospel, Jesus is made to make "a significantly formal repudiation of political ambition" (BJZ-318 f.). This is recorded in the course of his conversation with Pilate (John 18:36-37). Jesus declares here that his Kingship is "not of this world," but at the same time the "anti-Jewish" nature of John's thought also appears in Jesus' words to the effect that "if my kingship were of this world, my servants would fight, that I might not be handed over to the Jews."

Such, then, is the origin of the "pacific Christ" of the New Testament's Gospel.

"JESUS AND THE ZEALOTS"

This is the subject finally to be discussed, the title of the
book, and suggests the content of Brandon's thesis that
"Jesus and his movement did not constitute an isolated
phenomenon" (BJZ-356) in the Judaism of the first century. A real bond of understanding united the two move-
ments of Jewish Christianity as led by Jesus and the
Zealots with their allegiance to the "ideals of Judas of
Galilee" (BJZ-358). Jesus himself seems to have departed
from "Zealot policy" merely, not from Zealot idealism
(BJZ-356), in attacking the "sacerdotal aristocracy"
rather than the Romans directly. But there appears to be
nothing inappropriate that one so allied with the ideals of
Jewish nationalism should, like Judas of Galilee and his
two sons, die at the hands of their cause's enemies, and
that on either side of his cross with its title "The King of
the Jews" should die with him a *lestes,* the Romans' con-
temptuous title for a Zealot (BJZ-358).

This last chapter of the book constitutes a useful summary of Brandon's entire argument, and as this argument
is exceedingly detailed, the student might do well to read
this chapter first. We shall not, of course, follow our author in summarizing his argument, as we have endeavored
to do this with accuracy in this short account of his book.
Suffice it to say, then, that Mark, followed by the other
Evangelists for their own reasons, found it to the interests
of the Christian community to recognize Jesus as the Jewish Messiah whose career had been cut short by crucifixion. This was no doubt shocking in the extreme to them,
but by a distinctive interpretation of the O.T. Scriptures

they found plenty of warranty for the "sufferings of the Messiah"; once this was established and they had come to believe in Jesus' resurrection, they could also look for his return in short order to accomplish his mission as God's Messiah. This would eventuate in the restoration of the Kingdom to Israel, an event that necessarily implied the eventual overthrow of Judaism's enemies, including Rome (BJZ-324 f.).

We shall close our attempt to present Brandon's thesis by indicating several of the passages which he believes, when properly interpreted, give us an index to Jesus' person and motivation. Thus, he places Matt. 10:34 f. (Luke 12:51 f.)—"I came not to bring peace, but a sword"—among other passages which show that Jesus believed in "the use of force" (BJZ-20, 320n2). The verses immediately following (Matt. 10:35 ff.) are, he thinks, an "attenuating explanation . . . inspired by the primitive community's experience of what discipleship of Jesus meant in human relations." He chose a Zealot as a member of his disciple band (Simon); this does not mean that Jesus was himself a Zealot, but probably the opposite; it does mean, however, "that the profession of Zealot principles and aims was not incompatible with" joining forces with Jesus (BJZ-355). In fact, at the last in Gethsemane or just before his capture there, he "made sure that his disciples were armed" for the occasion (BJZ-340 f.). The fact that many Zealots had from time to time been crucified from A.D. 6 to 70 makes it appear likely that Jesus' saying about taking up one's cross and following after him was actually "probably of Zealot origin" (BJZ-344). Even Jesus' saying about "giving to Caesar" and "to God" that which belongs to each may have been what was approved by the Zealots with their ardent nationalism, for to them (and so to Jesus?) it would have been obvious that since "God owned the land of Israel," its fruitage and all its tribute must go to him alone (Mark 12:13-17; BJZ-345 ff.)!

As for the events of Passion Week, it opened with the so-called triumphal entry into Jerusalem—an action "designed to demonstrate his Messianic role" on Jesus' part (BJZ-350). This event was closely "followed by his attack on the Temple trading system," "a most radical challenge to the authority of the sacerdotal aristocracy" and as such also "a truly revolutionary act" (Mark 11:15 ff.; BJZ-332 f., 350). It was probably at this time that Jesus made some statement that led to his subsequently being accused of threatening to destroy the Temple (BJZ-234, 334). It is even likely that the cleansing of the Temple "was attended by violence and pillage" on the part of Jesus' confederates. Little wonder that "the Temple police either dared not intervene or were swept aside" (BJZ-333 f.)!

Such in brief is the image of the Jesus whom Brandon believes actually to have been the leader of a "para-Zealot movement," a nationalist of extreme type, and a proper colleague of assassins (*sicarii*) and brigands (*lestai*).

EVALUATION OF BRANDON'S JESUS, THE "PARA-ZEALOT" LEADER

Before we glance at Brandon's image of Jesus again with a view to its evaluation, it will be well to call the reader's attention to the fundamental difference between Brandon's and Schonfield's reconstructions of that image. In their endeavors to discover Jesus' niche in the Judaism of his day, they are one in concluding that it was as a "Jewish" Messiah that he was accepted by the Evangelists and that by and large the scope of his own motivation and aims was limited to the culture, demands, and salvation of the Judaism and the Holy Land to which he belonged. Any apparent widening of Jesus' outlook was in fact not his own, but rather that of the early church at some stage of its life and under pressures from without, such as that which Mark felt at Rome to widen the scope of Jesus' interests to include the Gentiles in his saving activities. (SPP-201 and BJZ-154, 237.)

But here the similarity ends. For Brandon, Jesus was prepared to employ violence because the image of the "Messiah" he accepted was essentially that of the Zealots and this meant such action on his part as "would end the domination of heathen Rome" (BJZ-218 f.). Schonfield holds, on the contrary, that "up to the time of Jesus the conception of a Warrior Messiah does not appear" (SPP-35). Pious Jews were awaiting rather a Messiah in terms of Isa. 11:4 and for such a one "the sharp two-edged sword of the Messiah would be no physical weapon, but justice and righteousness" (SPP-35). It is this genuine difference between these two authors that in the end makes their two positions to be worlds apart.

Similar likes and differences are to be seen among all five images thus far examined in this book. Although the authors employ the same tools of scholarship, yet start from differing standpoints of their own, the question may legitimately be raised which is the more important for the scholar's deductions—Jesus' *Sitz im Leben,* that of the church, or his own?

Accordingly, it is our thought that it would be apropos here to suggest several lines of argument of reflection that may be applied with equal cogency to all the books under review in the present volume, rather than to devote our space to Brandon's exhaustive work alone. We propose, indeed, to raise problems here rather than to endeavor in every case to arrive at a solution in the hope that the reader himself may wish to follow through to a more constructive solution than scholars have thus far proposed.

Without attempting an exhaustive list, let us examine the following questions that still need more airing than they have received:

First, it has been apparent in the discussion of Brandon's thesis how very much emphasis he places upon the matter of place, date, and *Sitz im Leben* of the writing of the canonical Gospels. Indeed, his thesis may be said to stand or fall in large measure with the idea that Mark wrote in Rome about A.D. 71. What if this is incorrect? What if Acts 13:5 ("they had John [Mark] as *hyperetes*") with the suggestion that Mark was *chazzan*, or custodian of their Christian Scriptures, gives us a better clue than Papias' *hermeneutes* of Peter for this young man? It would explain Paul's excessive anger at Mark's irresolution, if the meaning is that Paul was trying to stimulate him to write a "gospel" for the Greek churches. Who knew better than Paul of that need? And if, smarting under a tongue-lashing from Paul, at Syrian Antioch he came under Peter's kindly offices (Gal. 2:11 ff.), Papias might still not be too far out in the matter. At all events, if Mark wrote from Antioch, as there is some reason to believe, and possibly as early as A.D. 49 or 50, the entire picture is changed. This writer believes that a good case can be made out for this shift, leading to a quite different *Sitz im Leben* for Mark than Brandon supposes. In any case, the writer is not impressed with the idea that the so-called Latinisms of Mark are "weighty" reason for his writing in

Rome. Latin went all over the Empire with the Roman le-
gionnaire; Paul wrote to the "Romans" in Greek, not in
Latin; and in the second century a Latin Bible was called
for in North Africa before the Romans felt any such need.
A similar argument may be made out for Matthew and
Luke having been written elsewhere than in Alexandria
and Achaia respectively.

Secondly, is it good enough to suggest a *Sitz im Leben*
and to suppose that, given a strong motivation, one may
expect a given writer to respond to the situation as any
other similarly placed would do? The motivation Brandon
suggests at Rome of separating the Jewish Christians from
other Jews, to the betterment of the former in Roman
eyes, might or might not be sufficient for a Mark to be led
to sit down and write a Gospel that would show Jesus to
have been crucified because Pilate was, out of spite or
jealousy for their position, misinformed by the Jewish authorities. There is *a question of character, of holding to
truth whatever the cost may be,* to be considered.

Brandon himself, at this point in his argument, has referred to the case of Masada and Josephus' account of
what happened there—the only ancient historian to give
us any account whatever of the event (BJZ-24). Josephus'
relation to the event is remarkable, if for nothing else,
then for this—that, as Yigael Yadin has pointed out, this
Jewish historian had himself been one of the leaders of the
Zealots' "resistance movement" in Galilee at the outbreak
of the Jewish War of A.D. 66-73. He defected to the Romans, however, and later was called upon to write up the
history of his people for the Romans' enlightenment. Yet,
as Yadin remarks, "Whatever the reasons, whether pangs
of conscience or some other cause which we cannot know,
the fact is that his account is so detailed and reads so
faithfully . . . that it seems evident that he had been gen-

uinely overwhelmed by the record of heroism on the part
of the people he had forsaken" (Yigael Yadin, *Masada,*
1966; p. 15).

Is one, then, to understand that, given a set of circumstances and a prime need, any writer will write as any
other? Must there not rather be a "catalytic agent" in the
situation, composed of a given writer's character, motivation, or what not, and varying from one writer to another,
that will determine how close he will stick to the "facts"
and give us something of an objective tale? There is an old
saw to the effect that "the blood of the martyrs is the seed
of the church." Are we to understand that martyr-material
was not present in the earliest days of the church? It is not
good enough to reply that the Zealot cause had "religious"
overtones—no one denies this. (BJZ-355 f.) The question before us is this, Given a set of circumstances fraught
with great danger, such that "a man should sell his cloak
and buy a sword" if his mind works that way, *does, then,
every man's mind work that way? Did Mark's? Did Jesus'?
Do all men equally believe "violence" is the answer?*

Thirdly, this last leads us to remark on Brandon's em-
ployment of certain passages: "I came not to bring peace,
but a sword," that above from Luke about the "cloak" and
"sword" and its sequel where Jesus says, "It is enough,"
when told that there are "two swords" present in the disciple band (Luke 22:38). Brandon suggests that the latter
passage shows Jesus was concerned to see his disciples
"armed" (BJZ-317), that it is "scarcely likely" that the
number of swords is correctly reported and in any case
that the number is "immaterial" (BJZ-341). On the contrary, the number is deeply significant: "two swords"
against the might of Rome! For Jesus to have said that
this was "enough" is Luke's way of remarking that he had

his tongue in his cheek. Did Jesus never smile, was he never sarcastic or ironical? As for the first of the two passages above cited, it refers to family dissensions (Matt. 10:34 ff.; Luke 12:51 ff.) and the better text of Q in Luke does not even contain the word "sword."

Fourthly, once again one cannot but be impressed with Brandon's use of such phrases as "obvious," "unmistakable," "patently inadequate," "must," "likely," "probably," "obvious misrepresentation," "surely," "seems," "appears," "obscure," "incoherent," "manifestly absurd," and the like. A reasonable number of such words and phrases is to be expected of any author and no doubt most readers would disagree as to when that number had been reached. This writer for one can only record his own reaction to this book; the number has been so far exceeded as to suggest "special pleading" on the author's part. One acquires a sense of the "heads I win, tails you lose" technique being employed here. Particularly is this true perhaps when Brandon brings in the phrases "anti-Semitism" and "anti-Jewish" (BJZ-22, 226, 243, 248-256, 260-264, 265-280, 304, 310, 323), and the like. The church of the Dark and Middle Ages, and the Nazis in Germany, indulged in these attitudes, but are they to be seriously employed as explanations of the motivation of parties concerned in the crucifixion of Jesus? To my mind these expressions are *logical surds* and have no more place in Biblical criticism than their opposite—"anti-Goyim," "anti-Gentilism," "antipaganism," and the like.

Lastly, this writer should like to register his personal satisfaction in the fact that all five writers whose books we have thus far reviewed have expressed their own convictions clearly on the subject of Jesus' thought about himself. This is not an easy topic to deal with, and all the books reviewed have approached it with hesitancy. Yet, in the end, each writer has candidly stated his views on the subject of Jesus' probable self-awareness. This is, at least, a gain over the "blackout" on this subject which form criticism produced in the early days in many quarters. We need no longer be afraid to "psychologize" the historical Jesus in the name of a technique that endeavored to pull down a curtain over his mind.

6

The Church's Resurrected Lord

Günther Bornkamm's image of Jesus of Nazareth in his book by the same title is the first among those studied in this book which may legitimately be termed "Christian." This is not to say, of course, that for Bornkamm Jesus does not respect his Jewish heritage. That Jesus does so there can be no question. It is to say, rather, that Bornkamm views Jesus, not as a member of any category in the contemporary Judaism, but as one set apart and above, as one to whom no "customary or current conception" appears to apply, as one in a word distinctively Christian.

A quite cursory examination of this scholar's appraisal of the sects and groups within the Judaism of Jesus' day—the Pharisees, the Sadducees, the Samaritans, the Essenes, the Zealots—clearly shows his disapproval of any attempt to place Jesus in these categories. His summary statement about them contains the decisive dictum—"Jesus' message has nothing in common with these religious and political slogans" of such groups. But one of Jesus' contemporaries, in fact, approaches his spirit. This is, of course, John the Baptist (BJN-44).

There is yet another and deeper reason for labeling Bornkamm's image of the historic Jesus as "Christian" rather than as "Jewish" with those which have gone

before. This is the fact that throughout his book, he sees
Jesus' person, his words and actions to have been such as
to bring forth certain "repercussions" on the part of his
contemporaries (disciples and others) which, when developed, led to the church's faith in him as expressed by such
terms as "Messiah," "Son of Man," "Son of God," "Suffering Servant," and the like. In his statement of this phenomenon he declares he does not doubt that in all these
phrases with their genuine endeavor to glorify Jesus there
are to be found real "reactions and repercussions" to what
the historic Jesus was and said previous to the crucifixion.
Jesus' own statement to the effect that it was in his "person and work" that the Kingdom of God had "already
begun," together with the obvious fact that he felt a filial
relation toward God as his Father, a fact shown in many
of his sayings—all these things the church gathered up
and declared in the titles it gave him (BJN-174). To be
sure, as Bornkamm declares, Jesus never employed these
phrases with reference to himself. But the point we wish
here to emphasize is that for him the church's postresurrection claiming them for Jesus was the natural and logical
repercussion of what it had found him to be and teach.
That the church, then, should have employed these titles
in describing what Jesus was is right and proper, for so he
is in fact.

One further reference among many that could be made
will serve to point up Bornkamm's major position relative
to Jesus' person and the church's estimate of him. Writing
of the net result of all that he has thus far said, he remarks
of its "pre-eminently positive" nature and adds that Jesus'
character as Messiah is in actuality to be found "in" all he
says and does, indeed in what one may describe as the
"unmediatedness of his historic appearance." None of the
traditional categories as seen in Messianic title or function

which Jewish anticipation was prepared to apply to the
"Coming One" adequately describes Jesus' ministry, nor
does it "exhaust the secret of his being." No scribal or
other teaching within the circle of the preceding Judaism
can unlock for us the mystery of Jesus' person and work.
(BJN-178.)

So, among those scholars whose works we have been re-
viewing, Bornkamm is one set apart. Of Americans whom
one has read—in addition to James M. Robinson, like
Bornkamm a "Post-Bultmannian"—he should be placed
nearest to F. C. Grant and John Knox. Among Europeans,
he has of course learned most from Rudolf Bultmann, but
between him and this master there is a great gulf fixed.
Though this writer wrote nearly a quarter century before
Bornkamm, still he should even now find himself closer to
Bornkamm than to any other thus far studied, as one
imagines will appear to those who read Chapter 7 of this
book.

Our author gives us little to go on so far as his critical
methodology is concerned. He has an appendix on the Synoptic Gospels, their sources and history (BJN-215-220),
and another on the problem of Jesus' possible use of the
"Messianic titles" in referring to himself which helps us to
see how he would employ the standard critical methods of
the N.T. scholar (BJN-226-231). But, even in these ap-
pendixes and certainly everywhere else throughout the
book, methodology and the net product of its use are (in
view of his conscious and, therefore, intended purpose)
mingled together. This writer has no quarrel with this
artifice and has in fact used it at times, though the unini-
tiated or even stupid reader may sometimes be led astray
thereby. Recalling, then, at every step that Bornkamm so
approaches the Gospel data in his book, let us examine his
image of Jesus of Nazareth under this suitable heading.

BORNKAMM'S CRITICAL METHODS
AND THE RESULTING IMAGE OF JESUS

Our author devotes five chapters of his nine to this subject (Chs. 1, 3, 7, 8, and 9), Ch. 2 to the situation in the
contemporary Judaism, and the remainder (Chs. 4, 5, and
6) to Jesus' message. There are here at least two remarkable likenesses to Bultmann's outlining at which we have
looked in Chapter 2 above, as this occurs in both the master's *Jesus* and *Theology,* viz., Bornkamm like Bultmann
deals with Jesus' teaching in the order, first, "Kingdom of
God," and secondly, "Will of God"; and again, the study of
the "Messianic Question" and the nature of the person of
"Jesus Christ" comes *after* rather than *before* that of his
teaching (in Bultmann's case, in the *Theology* only),
though Bornkamm as we shall see has a better reason for
this ordering than Bultmann. Bultmann's further point on
"The Idea of God" in Jesus' teaching is incorporated by
Bornkamm under the section on the "Will of God," and
Bornkamm has a separate chapter on "Discipleship," the
like of which Bultmann could not well have as he thinks
the idea of appointing "the Twelve" arises in the early
church (BNTTh-37), a theory which Bornkamm cannot
accept (BJN-150).

These similarities between the two scholars' works are
more significant than might at first appear and it is this
significance alone that justifies the comparison. There is
no equivalent similarity between the writings of other
scholars working over these materials so far as this writer
can recall. The phenomenon testifies to the measure of accuracy to be found in the title given to what is perhaps the
dominant school of thought at the moment—the "Post-

Bultmannian school." As regards both methodology and net result, Bultmann has laid down the guidelines followed by this school of which one may perhaps speak of Bornkamm as its "father in God." We shall now address ourselves to a discovery of how far the school adheres to or contrariwise departs from the master's views, as far at any rate as this may be seen in Bornkamm's work.

On the whole, Bornkamm accepts the critical viewpoint of all modern historical scholarship which, so far as the Gospel history is concerned, finds it necessary to bypass the church's tradition and looking beyond it to attempt to view the events as they occurred (BJN-9). As regards the textual evidence and that of the sources behind the Gospels, he generally cites only what appears to be reliable, though this does not mean that apparently less reliable texts are necessarily so, nor that those cited were not also perhaps later creations of the church (BJN-11). All in all, Bornkamm does not rank himself on the side of "extreme scepticism" (BJN-10), and as one reads and ponders on his work, the impression becomes quite vivid that not nearly so much of the Gospel materials is "expendable" (to use Bishop Robinson's term) as is the case with Bultmann.

The Gospels according to Bornkamm present us with a combination of "faith" and "history" that is unique in the literature of the world. It was the church that wrote the Gospels and it did this after the experiences of the resurrection appearances. Everything in the Gospels is, therefore, written from the standpoint of the church's resurrection faith; Jesus is for the Evangelists to be sure a Nazorean scribe who lived in Galilee and died in Judea; but he is also the resurrected Christ and the bringer of redemption (BJN-16). The church, accordingly, looks at the historic Jesus from the standpoint of its resurrection faith. That is to say, everything that is to be found in our four Gospels has been written by men who believed in Jesus Christ as Lord and Savior; he is for them a rabbi (teacher, professor)—yes, but much more than a rabbi— he is above all else the resurrected, living Lord who is present by his Spirit in the church. Bornkamm even goes so far as to make the equation so dear to the heart of the average church member when he remarks: "These Gospels voice the confession: Jesus the Christ, the unity of the earthly Jesus and the Christ of faith. By this," he proceeds, "the Gospels proclaim that faith does not begin with itself but lives from past history." (BJN-23.)

This writer should like at this point to take space to break a lance with Bornkamm when he speaks of this post-resurrection view of Jesus Christ as something unique in the annals of historiography. He refers to "the bare facts as the modern historian reaches for them," to the "historical (in the usual sense)," to "what actually happened," to "what took place then and there," to "what was said then and there" (BJN-14 f.). And he does this with the intent of saying that the Gospels are different from all other historical writing because the authors of these Christian booklets have faith in the Person whom they portray, a resurrection faith that adds a subjective factor to what they write—a subjective factor the like of which is absent from all other historical writing.

This one cannot accept; for there is no historical writing in which the subjective factor(s) involving the author do(es) not play a part. The O.T. prophetic historians are a good example of this, but so is every modern historian of whatever school. To cite but two extreme examples: since 1918 we have been saying in the Western world that the Soviet writers were rewriting the history of discovery and invention so as to prove that all such have emanated from the skills and efforts of communistic scientists; and more recently in this country, the black movement has been charging that our histories all need rewriting to show what black men have done to advance our culture. The difference accordingly, between the Gospels and other historical writing does not lie in the presence or absence of a subjective factor added by the author(s). Rather, it is to be found in the exceptional nature of this particular subjective factor (the church's faith) and of the personality of the one on whom it impinges. And certainly, this difference, for the believer, works to the advantage of the essential historicity of the Gospels.

Bornkamm is on firmer ground as he writes of this essential historicity. For he disclaims any suggestion that we may glibly dismiss the church's tradition relative to Jesus of Nazareth as being "mere fancy or invention" and "as the mere product of imagination" (BJN-21). He admits the presence of "legends" and "legendary embellishments" in the Gospels (BJN-19), but denies the presence of "myth." "The Gospels are," indeed, he writes, "the rejection of myth." For, if there are "mythological conceptions" to be found in the church's faith, these always serve "the function of interpreting the history of Jesus as the history of God with the world" (BJN-23).

In consequence and, one might almost say as his final word on the subject of the authenticity of the picture of Jesus that we find in the Gospels, Bornkamm declares them to call for neither "resignation" nor "scepticism" on our part. The Jesus whom they present for our appraisal is without doubt the historic person of that name. The Gospels' account of Jesus' word and act, his life and ministry, is notable for its "authenticity," its "freshness," its "distinctiveness"—characteristics that impress one as genuine and quite unmarred by any excesses such as some would

look to find in the postresurrection faith of the church.
Rather, we are led to see in the Gospel image the genuine
historic Jesus as he was (BJN-24). It is in this light, then,
that we are to understand Bornkamm when he also writes
that at all levels the Gospel tradition about Jesus witnesses
to his historic actuality and to the certainty of his resurrection. Our constant endeavor, he says, must be to look for
the "history *in* the Kerygma" as presented by the Gospels,
and again "in this history" to find the Kerygma (BJN-21).

What, then, is the net result of this attitude toward the
Gospels and their sources, or perhaps better, their source
in the faith-motivated tradition of the postresurrection
church? And what sort of Jesus do we find portrayed in
the church's Gospels?

The answer to these questions Bornkamm gives us in
his third chapter. Here we find a wholly Jewish Jesus
about whose birth cluster a number of "legends" but of
whose "parents" and "brothers" forthright information is
given (BJN-53). He is a "rabbi" with no Greek philosophy or culture so far as we have any evidence. (BJN-54.)
His baptism by John fits into this Jewish picture and certainly occurred as narrated. But its meaning for Jesus cannot be known to us (BJN-54). The Gospels contain no
certain chronology, but they give us much of Jesus'
preaching and teaching, healing and other works. The
crowds are drawn to him, he makes disciples and enemies,
in the end he turns toward Jerusalem and there he is at
length to die.

Jesus belongs to the world of contemporary Judaism,
but "in the midst of it he is of unmistakable otherness"
(BJN-56). None of the customary Jewish "categories" fit
him. He is a "prophet," but more than a prophet, a
"rabbi," yet he "differs considerably from the other members of his class" (BJN-57). He speaks of God and the

world and men with a "directness" that sets him apart. The Gospels call this his "authority" (BJN-58), and he exhibits it in all his dealings with his disciples, his enemies, and all men. Bornkamm calls this sovereignty of the historical Jesus over every situation in which he is found "astounding," and so it is, indeed, for "every one of the scenes" that the Gospels portray for us exhibit this characteristic. It is found in his teaching, his healing, his dealing with demons, friends, and enemies! It all ends with Jesus on the cross, and this in a real sense is "the end of the world," or so the Gospels would have us understand (BJN-62)! It is the end, too, for all who have in any way been touched by this Jesus.

JESUS CHRIST: HIS OWN AWARENESS AND THE CHURCH'S FAITH

We need not linger long over Bornkamm's treatment of Jesus' teaching ministry for what it may contribute to his estimate of the Gospels' image of the Nazarene. His book, it is true, devotes three chapters to this theme. But much in these chapters recalls Bultmann's previous treatment. Like that scholar, he holds that Jesus' message is close to the contemporary eschatological views (BJN-66). Moreover, for Jesus, God's Kingdom is "already dawning" (BJN-67), so that "today" is the day of decision, and of this Jesus is the "sign" in his person and presence, but "not the thing itself." That is to say, Jesus does not embrace or replace the Kingdom but simply announces it as at hand and so to be received (BJN-69).

The Kingdom parables are generally told with a view to placing Jesus' auditors in anything but a position of mere "spectator" (BJN-74). They are in fact always God's call to "decision" (BJN-93). Jesus' teaching about the present and future in relation to the Kingdom, moreover, is not to be separated as though it referred to different eras or chronologically determined periods. Rather, the present dawning of the Reign of God is intended to suggest that one may expect "salvation and judgment" as its issue, while references to the "future" are meant to illuminate the mystery of the "present" as the "day of decision" (BJN-92).

Like Bultmann, Bornkamm also sees in Jesus' teaching about the will or demand of God a direct frontal attack on scribal casuistry and its emphasis on the law and legal righteousness (BJN-97, 105). With the scribe, obedience was something "measurable" (BJN-104), but what God wants is, as Bultmann phrased it, "radical obedience," or with Bornkamm, "a new righteousness." This is a matter of attitudes, of a new "state of being," a taking one's stand in decision for God (BJN-108).

As already remarked, Bornkamm believed that Jesus called out disciples, thereby exerting his own purpose to draw to himself the individual (BJN-145). This always pertained, both in the choice of the Twelve and in the calling of the larger group of fringe disciples (BJN-146). Unlike Bultmann, Bornkamm believes that Jesus appointed the Twelve, the number suggesting at once the original tribes that constituted God's old people, and also "the new people of God" in the eschatological times (BJN-150).

As regards the problem of the "Messiah secret" and the Wrede-Schweitzer "either-or" dilemma already discussed in Chapter 1, Bornkamm believes that there is a third way out of this apparent impasse. Neither may we, on the one hand, treat the secret as having been taught or invented by Jesus himself, nor on the other, may we hold that Jesus' ministry constituted "non-Messianic history" (BJN-171-172). The truth seems to lie between, and Bornkamm expounds it after this fashion. Let us begin by saying that "Jesus actually awakened Messianic expectations" by his various activities. This appears, not only as the "conviction" of his disciples "before his death," but also in the attitude of the authorities in Jerusalem and from "Pilate's verdict." From such clear indications, it seems that we should speak of "a movement of broken Messianic hopes . . . of one who was hoped to be the Messiah, but who . . . disappointed the hopes" thus resting on him (BJN-171-172)! That is to say, Jesus simply did not fulfill the Messianic image of the day, an image that his disciples along with the commonality of the day held. Nonetheless, let us hasten to say (with, indeed, a bit more haste than Bornkamm himself displays!) that there was every reason why those who heard Jesus should have had these hopes raised within their minds. For these hopes were the proper "reactions and repercussions of what we meet constantly in Jesus' word before his death" (BJN-174).

Let the reader reread the pages above, for in this statement of the case Bornkamm finds a *tertium quid datur* (a third way given), which really represents the fact of the matter as regards Jesus' attitude toward the "Messiah secret." And, we may repeat, in this third way he shows himself adopting a truly Christian interpretation of Jesus' ministry.

This is not to say, of course, that Bornkamm would accept at their face value such incidents as the baptism and temptations, the confession of Peter, and the like. Nor would he think of the birth narratives and the genealogies other than as legendary. All such materials in the Gospels represent the developed convictions of the church in the light of the resurrection appearances and their conviction of the oneness of Jesus of Nazareth with the Risen Lord and Christ. (BJN-173.) And the same conclusion must pertain relative to all the titles given to Jesus by others in the Gospels or apparently accepted or even expressed by himself of himself (BJN-174-178; App. 3). In the end, all such titles as applied to Jesus are found to represent the creeds and, of course, the theological views of the church (BJN-173).

Like Bultmann, Bornkamm again believes that the term "Son of Man," when used by Jesus of himself, never has the thought of suffering, death, and resurrection attaching to it. These ideas come out of Jesus' "experience" and are elaborated by the church in whose later tradition the final account of Jesus even altered the cast of his teachings (BJN-177). By then also, the term "Son of Man" had been wholly equated with "Jesus" and so was quite capable of being "interchanged" with this historic name in the church's thought and speech.

Finally, as regards the events of Passion Week and beyond them in the resurrection—here again it is correct to speak of Bornkamm as taking a mediating position, one imagines. Quite contrary to the position later to be elaborated by Brandon, he remarks of Jesus' "express refusal" to take up with the Zealots' political aspirations (BJN-66). In opposition to the suggestion of Schonfield and others also that Jesus was the "Jewish Messiah," though without specific reference to their views, he writes that Jesus' ministry and efforts generally are not to be thought as specifically traditionally Messianic in character and so not as against the Roman authority (BJN-153). Jesus went up to Jerusalem for this closing week of his life simply and solely because it was for him "the city of God" and so there, too, he must preach "the gospel of the Kingdom"—

in this city so intimately related to Israel's past and future (BJN-154).

However we are to view such incidents of Passion Week as the so-called "triumphal entry" and the Temple's cleansing, it is instructive to note that all the Gospels raise here the problem of the nature of Jesus' "authority" on these occasions. This is well-advised (BJN-159). Nonetheless, we still fall back, Bornkamm holds, on Jesus' thought that it is in his teaching that God's Kingdom may be said to be "dawning" and that every man's "decision," therefore, relates ultimately to himself. Here, so far as we can clearly see, the matter of Jesus' claims about himself will have to rest. Jesus is eventually sentenced to death "for blasphemy" according to the Gospels, though there is no single like case on record in Jewish annals. Actually, Luke and John represent Jesus as handed over by the Jewish authorities to Pilate as one suspected to be politically culpable, and so far their report of the matter is no doubt quite correct (BJN-164, 165).

As regards the resurrection, Bornkamm is very explicit about his belief that it was "appearances" (reportedly of a Jesus risen from the dead) and the testimony of those who saw them that gave rise to the Easter faith, rather than the reverse in any sense. The "Easter stories," it is true, are to be taken as "evidence of the faith" of the disciples that Jesus had risen; moreover, they contain much in the nature of "legend" and are not "records and chronicles" of what exactly happened. It is true, too, that "the *message* of Easter" is to be sought in these stories. Nonetheless, let no one imagine or conclude that the "message" is the "product" of the believing church. For, the appearances were prior to the faith, not the faith to the appearances (BJN-183). It is, then, the resurrected Lord who speaks in the Gospels and through the church, and one may say with confidence that "the Church has its origin and its beginning in the resurrection of Jesus Christ" (BJN-186).

APPRECIATIVE APPROACH TO BORNKAMM'S IMAGE OF JESUS CHRIST

It is difficult, one imagines, to praise Bornkamm's book too highly. Here, indeed, is *a* way—possibly *the* way—for the scholar to find a path through the wilderness of the Bultmannian *Formgeschichte* to the Promised Land of the church's faith. And though here and there signs remain of the "red herring" of existentialism that the master drew across the Gospel landscape, the categories with which they are surrounded are quite Biblical, as, one believes, are the residual deposits themselves. "Myth," too, appears to have been summarily dismissed by Bornkamm.

Accordingly, for our critique of Bornkamm's position, it will perhaps be well for us to be as "pre-eminently positive" in our approach as he declares himself to be in his deductions from the Gospel data. To this end, we call attention to four principles of interpretation which appear to us to cover fairly the ground of Bornkamm's dealing with these data.

First, wherever there appears to be *unresolved tension* between the church's developed belief and what is reported in its written Gospels, here we may feel relatively certain that we are treading on historic ground. To take one good example of the working of this interpretative principle—Jesus' baptism at the hand of John the Baptist. This event presented various difficulties for the church: (*a*) "the Messianic baptiser is one to be baptised, the judge of the world is among the sinners"! (*b*) "strong ten-

sion" also exists between the church's view of the Christ as
Savior and John's representing him to be almost if not
quite exclusively as "judge" with "winnowing fork" in
hand; then, (c) there is the absence of any reference in
the Gospel to "a separate individual sect" grouped about
John rather than Jesus (BJN-46-48). In these various
ways, the story of Jesus' baptism furnished the church
with difficulties, yet it maintained it in the tradition and reported it in the written Gospels. This fact speaks to us of
the church's veracity in this and like traditions. Nonetheless, this same church tradition has "transformed the story
into a testimony to the Christ," namely, through the
speaking of the voice from heaven and the vision reported
as seen by our Lord only. Hence, we are not entitled to
conclude from the account "what baptism meant for Jesus
himself, for his decisions and for his inner development"
(BJN-54).

Secondly, relative to the matter of Jesus' consciousness
of mission, we have already seen that Bornkamm holds
the later church's "exalted titles" for Jesus to be legitimate
"reactions and repercussions of what we meet constantly
in Jesus' word before his death" (BJN-174). Add to this
principle of interpretation the observation made above:
"The Messianic character of his being is contained *in* his
words and deeds and *in* the unmediatedness of his historic
appearance" (BJN-178); and the equally striking depar-
ture made by Bornkamm from Bultmann's view on the appointment of the Twelve: the one holding that Jesus made
this appointment, the other that the idea is one created by
the church (BJN-150)—and one begins to wonder what
is left to be desired in the matter of Jesus' self-awareness of
Messiahship in some sense!

Thirdly, as seen in the tale of the two on the way to
Emmaus told by Luke (Luke 24:13 ff.), "it is the resur-

rected Christ," Bornkamm contends, "who first reveals the mystery of his history and his person, and above all the meaning of his suffering and death" (BJN-185). He makes much of this incident as determinative of the church's own view of the matter, returning to it again and again, though there are other passages that essentially say the same thing, or at least when added together, may be so understood (Mark 9:9; Luke 24:8; John 2:2; 12:16; 14:26). It is, then, the Spirit of Truth, the Spirit of the resurrected Jesus Christ, who communicates to his church the meaning of his life and ministry, his death and resurrection. And it is the Word of this same Spirit which we find in the Gospels, illuminating each incident in the life with the light of its meaning for the God of history. (BJN-191.)

Fourthly, none of the titles of majestic significance that the church throughout its history and among any people has assigned to Jesus in its creeds and confessions retains the old meaning unchanged. This is true no matter what its source, whether Jewish or Hellenistic. (BJN-190.) Messiah, Son, Son of David, Son of God, Son of Man, Lord—all of these "take on the mystery of his person and history, and acquire a new sense." This is because in every case "the confession of the disciples is the answer to the act of God and to the word which went forth in Jesus Christ" (BJN-191).

There can be no question, one imagines, that these four interpretative principles of Bornkamm serve to bring the Jesus of history closer to the Christ of the church's faith than any presentation that we have thus far described in these pages. Still, questions like these seem to remain unanswered. If the account(s) of any or of all experiences of Jesus of Nazareth cannot tell us what these "meant for

Jesus himself," then can we be sure that we are really in touch with him in Bornkamm's interpretation?

And then, does this not seem to contradict the principle of "repercussions"? Surely, such repercussions were from what the incidents "meant for Jesus himself," and if so, it was what the church sensed of all this that led to the same. If this is not so, then was the church not self-deceived rather than led by the Spirit as Bornkamm otherwise maintains?

Again, we may ask, who was it that selected just the titles found in the Gospels as aptly applying to Jesus? For it does seem that *a selective process* was here at work, and if we follow Bornkamm, there was also *a defining process* operating in the Gospels' pages. Were these developments the work of the church, of the Spirit guiding the church, or even of the historic Jesus? Or, in view of the "repercussions" view, are we to think of all three sources as one eventually? And if so, are we to say there was no hint of these developments before the resurrection?

7

The Prophetic Suffering
Servant-Messiah

In April, 1943, William Manson and this writer, on opposite sides of the Atlantic, published two books with
substantially the same thesis, though neither was aware
that the other was writing on the subject. His book was
called *Jesus the Messiah,* the other, *The Intention of
Jesus.* His view is evident in a passage in which he is discussing "Son of God" as a proper title to apply to Jesus of
Nazareth; here he remarks that the evidence "forces to the
front the question *whether we are not to seek in the depths
of Jesus' own spirit the source and origin-point of this particular form of the Christian Messianic idea."* (MJM-
150). Note his stress on the "Christian" view of a Messiah. Similarly, the thesis of *The Intention of Jesus* is:
*"Jesus and he alone was reponsible for the fusion of the
two prophetic concepts . . . and everything he ever said
or did was motivated by his 'intention' to fulfill the demands of the resultant Suffering Servant, Messiah of the
Remnant concept."* (BIJ-2.)

The point is that both these writers look to the self-
awareness of Jesus as a datum that may be seen and
investigated through and behind the thick glass of the
church's tradition as seen in our canonical Gospels. The
reason for the importance of this investigation into the

"mind of the historic Jesus" is evident from the pages that have gone before in this book. And it is perhaps not too much to say that the thesis of these two books was as distinctive in its day as any other that we have examined. These writers were followed by a number of others whose views relative to Jesus Christ and his conscious meaning for human life differ only in matters of detail. Several of these may be listed as follows: Oscar Cullmann, *Baptism in the New Testament* (1950; pp. 12-22); Vincent Taylor, *The Gospel According to St. Mark* (1952; pp. 122 ff.); C. H. Dodd, *According to the Scriptures* (1953; pp. 110, 114 ff.); T. W. Manson, *The Servant-Messiah* (1953; p. 36); W. G. Kümmel, *Promise and Fulfilment* (1957; pp. 109-121); and others.

These writers differ in their methods of approach to the problem, in their allegiance to the findings of form criticism and the work of the school of Comparative Religions, in the use of terms such as "myth" and "existentialism," and in the value they attach to research in the apocalyptic literature and the Dead Sea Scrolls and the like. *But they are one in their belief that the church has accurately portrayed the mind of Jesus Christ in its Gospels,* to the general effect that he knew himself to be the fulfillment of the inspired imagination of Hebrew prophecy and the Mediator of the salvation God has for mankind universally. For, though admittedly in the Gospels we have in the first instance the church's presentation of Jesus Christ as it viewed him, a la Bornkamm in the light of his resurrection and the faith that event engendered in it, *yet there is no a priori reason why this view of him may not be accurate or why it may not correspond with his own.*

It is the contention of these writers that the church's view is by and large accurate and that it emanates from Jesus about himself. It will be the purpose of this final chapter to show why this is so; and, to simplify a very complex problem, we shall in general present the case as it is to be found developed in *The Intention of Jesus,* supplementing at some points from the work of others. As regards *methodology,* there are but three points that are perhaps of most importance: first, "the *critical* approach to the New Testament's literary and historical problems" is accepted at every turn and underlies the entire argument (BIJ-4); secondly, with William Manson I accept the principle made evident by research that "the community remembered better than it understood" (MJM-32), or as I have stated the same, "The evangelists . . . in some instances even appear to be unaware of the significance of the very events which they report" (PCB-736); thirdly, the undoubted fact is to be borne in mind that "actions speak louder than words," and that, accordingly, it may be assumed that so great a one as Jesus will reveal himself best in slight word or hint or gesture or action, even indeed in the questions he asks of others. All of these seem to the present writer to add up to the conclusion just stated that *"everything he ever said or did was motivated by his 'intention' to fulfill the demands of the resultant Suffering Servant, Messiah of the Remnant concept"* (BIJ-2).

DEVELOPMENT OF THE ARGUMENT
FROM *The Intention of Jesus*

In several ways the point has already been made that the creators of five of the images of Jesus appearing in this book seem to imagine it a foregone necessity for Jesus of Nazareth to be categorized according to one or other of the existing groups in the Judaism of his day. The problem these authors have set for themselves is the rather simple one of discovering to which of these he belonged. But the fact that all the groups available (with the exception of the Sadducees) have in turn been found acceptable appears to cancel out all such attempts. *Jesus of Nazareth simply does not fit the requirements of any known Jewish group of his day.*

Accordingly, it is the contention of the writers reviewed in this chapter that the question of Jesus' spiritual and moral climate is to be approached from the standpoint of the Scriptural substratum which all contemporary groups acknowledged. This is the prophetic scripture known to us as the Old Testament, the Hebrew Bible accepted basically by all Jews in Jesus' day as the work of the ancient prophets who had been inspired by the Living God.

The frontispiece chart indicates the common source book of all the contemporary Jewish groups, i.e., the prophetic Scriptures of the Old Testament, together with the various groups that drew from its treasures and the modern authors who have placed Jesus somewhere among these groups. Bornkamm alone of the writers thus far examined is unsatisfied with these findings, holding that the church following the resurrection performed a creative act in finding for Jesus *a new, non-Jewish category—one responding by way of "repercussions" to what even in preresurrection days it had discovered in him but only now in the light of his resurrection was able to formulate.*

What, then, is left for the writers presently under review in this chapter to say? Only this—that for the past twenty-five years we have been endeavoring to underline the facts and the nature of the facts to which the church's "repercussions" were made. To state the matter very bluntly—we have contended that Jesus at no time would have been found "in character" had he stepped out into the marketplace or the Temple and shouted out: "Look at me! I am the Messiah, the Son of Man, the Suffering Servant," or any like title for himself. Rather, by word and deed, everything he ever said or did simply added up to what these words may mean. Of this he was always cognizant; so as he went about as Mediator of the Kingdom of God to men, he did not have to be continually stating his case; he had merely to go on *being* these things, thereby challenging all his contemporaries in one way or another to *see* them for themselves and to make the *believing response* they were calculated to inspire.

It was so, we believe, that *Jesus bypassed all of contemporary Judaism, going back rather to the prophetic Scriptures afresh and by a process of selectivity creating a totally new image of the Mediator God wished for men.* This image was new for the reason that never before had it remotely occurred to anyone in the Hebrew-Jewish tradition to combine such figures as "Messiah," "Son of Man," "Suffering Servant," "Son of God"—all of these old and well-worn while each remained aloof from the others, but creatively new and exciting when brought together and even more lived out in the experience of one individual, Jesus of Nazareth.

THE CHURCH'S SOLUTION—JESUS, THE SUFFERING SERVANT-MESSIAH

This is the formula which the church incorporated in its first written Gospel, that of Mark, at its account of Jesus' baptism (Mark 1:9-11), for the heavenly voice is here made to quote from Ps. 2:7 ("You are my son") and Isa. 42:1 ("my beloved" or "my chosen," "with thee I am well pleased"). This double quotation, it is rather generally recognized, is intended by Mark to create of these two parts a sort of *coronation* (Messiah)*-ordination* (Suffering Servant) formula. This formula is intended by the Gospel writer to redefine the nature of Messiahship in terms of suffering servanthood. So much may surely be said without unduly misjudging the consensus of modern N.T. scholarly opinion, though there are, it is true, occasional dissenting voices.

The *real problem* involved in this passage and incident concerns, therefore, *how far the church's interpretation corresponds to Jesus' own mind about the matter*. It is this which constitutes the problem to which *The Intention of Jesus* seeks the answer—an answer recorded in the quotation from this book, above (BIJ-2). Briefly, the various points in the argument may be stated as follows:

DID JESUS INTEND TO LIVE OUT THE SUFFERING SERVANT-MESSIAH IMAGE?

This, we believe, was indeed his intention, and in so stating the church through its Evangelists reported his purpose accurately. We begin, as just indicated, with Jesus' baptism for the reason that the authenticity of an account representing the church's Lord as coming to a baptism "of repentance for remission of sins," and that at the hand of one who might accordingly be considered as his superior, is self-evident; such an incident created difficulties for the church to explain or explain away!

But, that the baptism has evidential value for Jesus' view of the matter is also clear.

First, an examination of all four Gospels makes it appear that the church's earliest tradition held that Jesus alone saw the heavenly vision and heard the heavenly

voice on this occasion. This means but one thing, viz., that
the experience was internal to the mind or spirit of Jesus
only (BIJ-35 ff.). If this is so, it is but one step farther
to observe that he also must, then, have understood its
meaning. *"Voices from heaven"* in Scripture "are heard
only by those equipped to *hear* them!" (BIJ-36.) Jesus
heard this voice because he was ready for it, and if ready,
then he understood it, and if he understood it, then he
knew himself the Suffering Servant-Messiah it proclaimed
—so runs our argument.

If a time or date is sought when Jesus might well have
reported all this to his disciples, then that would naturally
be after Peter's confession, when by all accounts he took a
step in advance in his teaching of them (Mark 8:31 ff.).
That would also be the date when he would tell them of
the nature of his temptations where he had been placed on
the horns of the dilemma—whose Messiah should he be,
God's or Satan's, a spiritual leader of men or a political
figure seeking popular acclaim? (BIJ-40, 160-167).

Secondly, from the very beginning of his ministry, Jesus
of Nazareth must have been confronted with the question
of cultural affiliation, Where should he take his stance
within the society of his day? Where, indeed, should John
the Baptist take his? Where should any spiritual leader
stand? Or, should he, like the old prophets stand alone,
speaking his piece like Micaiah ben Imlah as God placed
it in his mouth? (I Kings 22:14.)

Since the discovery of the Dead Sea Scrolls some four
years after *The Intention of Jesus* was written, one need
no longer argue that the Judaism of Jesus' day was not the
unified phenomenon that some scholars have held. The
"Faith of Israel" had never been a single creed uniformly
accepted; the writings of the Hebrew prophets are replete
with the scandalous beliefs and practices against which

they declaim their jeremiads, and for the first century of our era, Josephus (himself a Jew) is all the evidence one should require to discover the division and dissension within the Jewish culture of his firsthand acquaintance.

That Jesus was aware of all this needs no proof. But Ch. II in *The Intention of Jesus* has been devoted to say so at a date (1943) when the scrolls were not yet known, and it has also been pointed out that *"the prophetic voice in the Hebraic culture"* at all periods was *"a thing apart"* (BIJ-69). This "voice," too, "had a doctrine of its own of the Messiah, one not to be confused with either the particularistic, racial Messiah of popular Pharisaism, or the supramundane 'Son of Man' Messiah of the apocalyptic literature," or, it may now be said, the Aaronic Messiah or the somewhat enigmatic "Teacher of Righteousness" of the Essene sect (BIJ-71). For, "in the *prophetic strand* of the Hebraic culture the concepts of *universalism* . . . and *Messiahship* emerged and grew apace in the minds of the same prophets," as did also "the concept of the Remnant which gradually succeeded in breaking down the idea that Israel stood related to God *as a unit.* . . . It became clear that a man stood related to God on an individual level. . . . His membership in the Remnant became a matter, not of racial ties, but of *a moral choice!* . . . The *universalization* of the idea of man's religious relation to God of necessity follows its *individualization"* (BIJ-72 f.). That all of this is true must certainly follow from a study of a host of passages in Isaiah, Hosea, Amos, Micah, and then in Jeremiah, Zephaniah, Deutero-Isaiah, Zechariah, and the like (BIJ-245n83).

Coming, then, from a fresh reading of the Hebrew prophets with these concepts of a spiritual-moral leader ("the prophet," "the Messiah," "the Branch," "the Servant of Yahweh" who suffers to save), of the faithful remnant, of the individual standing quite alone before God and so bereft of the security to be found in the race or nation, and in consequence of a universalism that must eventuate when such racial solidarity is no more in the picture, one realizes for the first time what a wealth of material lay to hand for one like Jesus to sort out and so create an utterly new image of the universal Messiah of a remnant that should include all peoples within its bounds. It becomes intelligible, therefore, as C. H. Dodd has said (DAS-110), that Jesus felt prompted to do just that, the result being, as Bultmann has well said, that "the Jewish concept Messiah-Son-of-Man" was "singularly enriched" by the new combination of prophetic ideas never before brought together, "as the idea of a suffering, dying, rising Messiah or Son of Man was unknown to Judaism" (BNTTh-31). Bultmann, of course, thinks this enriching fertilization of the Messiah concept was accomplished, not by Jesus, but by the later church. But, with what right does Bultmann conclude that any reference to passion on Jesus' lips must be a *vaticinium ex eventu?* Certainly, it is far more likely that this enrichment would emanate from one as creative as Jesus than from any other of whom we have any knowledge. *Ideas are as powerful agents as are events to stimulate the creative mind, and the man of prophetic stature has never required to learn a lesson from history* ex eventu.

Accordingly, we have concluded that Jesus simply bypassed all contemporary Jewish groups, going back to the prophetic Scriptures for what stimulus he required, and like Schweitzer and Schonfield, each in his way, we have long since come to believe that Jesus set before himself a reconstructed image of Messiahship, one of a highly spiritual and moral type, universalistic and so nonracial in character. This, we believe, is what the Gospels in their several ways are endeavoring to say to us, and like C. H. Dodd we see no real reason for disbelieving them!

Thirdly, it is our contention that there is a "certain pattern of consistency" which is seen to "emerge in Jesus' ministry and teaching. This pattern of consistency is not one which we should expect of lesser men than Jesus of Nazareth. There is 'a type of consistency that is the logic of fools,' but there is also a type that because of its depth of insight gives us a picture of a mind possessed of vast, even universal, comprehensiveness" (PCB-736). This consistency should, and we believe did, take in Jesus' entire activity of word and deed throughout his ministry.

It is now generally recognized that we cannot trace development either in Jesus' mind or in his activities. What he was, what he thought, what he taught, what he intended —all these are, so far as may be discovered, one from beginning to end of his career. The consistency of which we speak is the hallmark of this fact—Jesus' every act and teaching are somehow to be seen as comprising, or better, expressing a unity of intention that is surprising, to say the least. Accordingly, we have made strong objection to Maurice Goguel's amazing statement that Jesus never considered his marvelous works "essential." "Quite the contrary, Jesus' 'mighty works' either were thoroughly integrated with his teaching and preaching, indeed, with his life's mission and activity as a whole, or else to his mind they ceased to serve any useful function." (BIJ-113.)

Accordingly, it becomes possible to remark with Bornkamm that Jesus' every act is as it were an epitome in miniature of his entire ministry. Nothing that Jesus is recorded to have either said or done is lacking in this quality of consistency.

There is no better example of this than his choice of the

Twelve. There appear to be at least two independent accounts of this: one in Mark, the other in Luke's "special
source." The first of these is interlarded by Mark with rising controversy with the Pharisees (Mark 1:16 ff.; 2:13 ff.;
2:1-12; 2:18 to 3:6; 3:13 ff.; 5:1 ff.; 6:1-6), which
ends with Jesus' expulsion from the synagogue in "his
own country." The other begins with the rejection at Nazareth (Luke 4:16-30) and proceeds immediately to the
call of four disciples (ch. 5:1-11), then to that of Levi
(vs. 27 f.), and finally to the choice of the Twelve as a
whole (ch. 6:12 ff.). There is obvious overlapping in the
two accounts, but the essential point is clear, viz., that
*for both, controversy and final rejection form the back-
ground of Jesus' appointment of the Twelve.* (BIJ-Ch. VI,
esp. 215 ff.)

From this twofold witness, we have argued that Jesus'
appointment of the Twelve is somehow to be related to his
rejection from the assembly of his people. And, moreover,
when we note that in both sources (Mark and L) Jesus
never again darkens the door of a synagogue, the point
seems to become clear that for him this extirpation was
final; so that he *now conceives it his duty to begin to build
up a new assembly of God's people, starting from the
Twelve as a "remnant" to form the new "people of God,"*
what in later times was termed the "Church." (BIJ-219 ff.)

There is much more to be said in support of this suggestion. For example, it was not the custom of either prophet
or rabbi in the Hebrew-Jewish ethos to choose disciples.
Moses and Elijah, by express command of God, chose
theirs—a highly exceptional action on their part. John the
Baptist is an exemplar of the general rule. He took his disciples as they came to him, merely objecting to some as
being unworthy, but not endeavoring to stimulate any to
come to baptism or discipleship by way of preference to

others (Luke 3:7 ff.). Jesus is, therefore, a notable exception to this rule; he both chose his disciples and when he reached twelve, he stopped making such choice. The number twelve, accordingly, was significant for him, as it was for Peter and presumably for the others (Acts 1:21 f.). Similarly, the number "about a hundred and twenty" was significant for Luke (Acts 1:15), that is, twelve times ten, the number which according to Jewish tradition could stand for Israel as a whole (M. Sanhedrin 1:6), ten being the number of male adults who could represent a unit, or tribe, hence a congregation, within Israel. A hundred and twenty, accordingly, would stand for the "new Israel" or a quorum of the same and so be capable of doing business. *And the point is that the two sources in Mark and Luke trace this general type of thinking back to Jesus and his activity.*

Fourthly, the term "Son of Man," as most scholars including Bultmann are agreed, is to be traced back to Jesus for its use with reference to himself. The problem is, therefore, not whether Jesus employed the phrase, but what he meant by it; and Bultmann, followed by others, believes he employed it of himself only as the equivalent of " 'man' or 'I' " (BNTTh-30), or as in English we might say "one," e.g., one says, one thinks, etc. Bornkamm appears to go beyond Bultmann at this point in declaring quite unequivocally, "I consider it probable that the historical Jesus never used the title 'Son of man' for himself" (BJN-230). In the light of the evidence presented from all the Gospel sources in *The Intention of Jesus* (180 and 203), one cannot but be surprised at this conclusion of Bornkamm. It is one thing to dispute the sense in which a phrase is employed; it is quite something else to deny its use at all in the face of overwhelming evidence to the contrary.

This writer believes that the phrase "Son of Man" on Jesus' lips, when used of himself, is of a piece with all the others of his words and deeds to which Bornkamm finds the church reacting (his theory of "repercussions"). Jesus never says, as remarked above: "Look at me! I'm the Messiah." What he does is to call men to "follow" him and then to open their eyes and see for themselves what there is about him that should command their attention. "Having eyes," he asks them, "see ye not? and having ears, hear ye not? and do ye not remember?" (Mark 8:18, KJV). "When the disciples of John the Baptist inquire of Jesus whether he is the 'coming one,' the reply is, 'Go and tell John the things which ye have seen and heard.'" (BIJ-170.) The implication is—you must look at the evidence and make up your own minds on that basis. Mark, in fact, never discloses for his readers what it is that the disciples were to hear and see in the above passage; possibly he did not himself know! The Fourth Gospel, too, follows out this same pattern in Jesus' dealings with those about him (John 1:39, 46).

"Son of Man," then, on Jesus' lips will have been of the same nature. This phrase had a lengthy history behind it and could be employed in several ways: (a) with Ezekiel as God's stock phrase in addressing his prophet, (b) as the proper way to refer to an individual man in both Hebrew and Aramaic, (c) in Dan. 7:13 ff. to stand for the "people of the Most High" collectively—they to whom the eternal kingdom was committed, (d) in the "Similitudes" of Enoch (I Enoch 37-71) possibly to stand for this people *collectively* and also for their great Leader, the Messiah *individually*. So with Jesus, in line with his observed reticence about referring to himself, *the phrase may very well have served his enigmatic purpose of challenging men to make up their own minds about him.*

In this writer's judgment, Jesus' use of "Son of Man" of himself is exactly in line with his usual practice of calling forth spiritual expression from others. He employs a phrase of himself that may mean many things and he thereby challenges those within the sound of his voice to fill it with whatever content they will! Perhaps its nearest equivalent on his lips would be that of the Persian *banda* (humble servant), a term commonly employed in ordinary conversation as in English we should say "one" with reference to oneself, *but with a history implying reticence, reserve, even the purpose to demean oneself* (as in Ezekiel?); and so with Jesus of himself "Son of Man" may be quite possibly the equivalent of "servant" (of Yahweh). This is the more likely, one imagines, inasmuch as Jesus nowhere employs the phrase "servant of Yahweh" or "suffering servant" of himself, though in a number of disputed passages in which he is made to speak of himself, the term "Son of Man" appears with the "humiliation" motif (BIJ-143).

In the light of the phrase's history as just indicated, it is not surprising that Jesus should have employed it in passages in which the *exaltation* motif similar to Dan. 7:13 ff. and 1 Enoch 37-71 is present. *"What was new with him was that to the Son of Man, Messiah concept he brought the motif of humiliation, of suffering and death!"* That is, before the Gospels, there is no record of the *humiliation* motif being attached to the phrase "Son of Man." If, then, Jesus did not originate this phenomenon, who did?

To reply that the church did this in the light of the cross is hardly good enough. It *is* intelligible that Paul in that light should attach the idea of suffering to the term "Messiah," as he does in I Cor. 1:23 and 2:2; it is *not* intelligible that the church should similarly go out of its way to pervert the meaning of "Son of Man," a phrase with a history that was already confusing enough! But to make matters doubly confusing it is proposed by some that the church employed its inventive skill in adopting the phrase of Jesus—and that in the *humiliation* sense that had never attached to it—and *then at once said that it was he, not itself, that had so employed the phrase.* Even Paul did not attempt to do this with the term "Messiah," and this writer confesses he finds it impossible to accept.

As regards the other "Son" passages in the Gospels (including those recorded so frequently in the Fourth Gospel), this writer should be prepared to go beyond Bornkamm in applying his "repercussion" theory to them as well, again after the manner indicated in the several paragraphs above (BJN-App. 3, p. 226). It has been observed by many students of the Gospels that Jesus' sense of filial relation to his Father was one of the marked features of his life. (BJN-174.) Indeed, it is possible that his usual address of God in prayer was the simple "Father" (Luke 11:2), and this because the single word expressed the whole of the intimate fellowship involved. Is more than this really involved in such a passage as the Q saying at Matt. 11:25-27 and Luke 10:21 f.? And may it not be that it is this which lies behind all the "Son-Father" passages in John's Gospel? It is always easy to read too much into the text of a passage in order to proceed at once to read it out, the true meaning being overlooked in both procedures!

The long history of the relationship between God and man recorded in the Old Testament includes many uses of the terms "son" and "Father" to define the same. Some of these have reference to mankind generally in his relation to God, some to Israel in an exclusive sense of sonship, some to the individual within Israel, some even to heavenly beings (Gen. 6:2, 4; Ex. 4:22 f.; Hos. 11:1; Ps.

89:26 f.; Isa. 43:6). The passage in John 10:34 f. (Ps. 82:6) is one of those whose meaning is quite enigmatic but may serve to show the process of "repercussion" to Jesus' actual saying about himself at work.

Is there, then, any reason why Jesus may not have employed the term "Son" of himself as he spoke of his "Father," seeing that it had this rich background in the prophetic Scriptures? This is by no means to say that in doing so he was meaning what the church's creeds have meant by "Son of God," nor is it to say that those creeds' Greek meaning was the way the church's doctrine should have developed. It is merely to remark that the Evangelists accurately describe Jesus as employing the terms "Son" and "Father" in the religious sense, and relative to his relation to God. To go farther and really sound the depth of what he meant by the terms, perhaps we should follow somewhat the same method as that adopted in connection with the phrase "Son of Man," or it may even be that for the time being we should confess ourselves as quite beyond our depths and await more light to break. This writer is satisfied to say that he believes Jesus to be rightly understood as meaning that his relation to God was of a unique (*monogenes*) character. The church understood this to be the case and it responded accordingly with a unique faith in him.

THE EVENTS OF PASSION WEEK AND BEYOND

Finally, this writer has long since written of his general agreement with Schweitzer when he speaks of Jesus being in complete control of the situation during Passion Week. His elaboration of this thesis is summarized above in Chapter 1. Schonfield, too, agrees with this viewpoint,

though the twist he gives to the argument relative to Jesus'
contemplation of assumed death and resurrection constitutes no part of what Schweitzer wrote.

a. The so-called "triumphal entry" into Jerusalem on
Jesus' part was rather one of humiliation, for he was
merely received as any "prophet" would have been (Matt.
21:11), or indeed as all pilgrims were, with the singing of
the antiphonal Ps. 118 (BIJ-149 f.); but the account
makes it clear that Jesus is here challenging the capital
city to accept him as Messiah in some sense (Zech. 9:9;
Matt. 21:4-5), and that he had made his arrangements accordingly with care (Mark 11:2-6). The church came to
see this only after the resurrection, as Bornkamm's thesis
suggests (John 12:16), but the more this is so the more it
becomes apparent that the preresurrection Jesus had been
acting after a fashion to call forth the postresurrection
church's reaction of astounding faith in him.

b. The cleansing of the Temple was equally staged by
Jesus with a view to challenging its Sadducaic authorities
with a claim that was above theirs in this sacred place; for
the Talmud calls the Temple markets "the bazaars of the
sons of Annas," that is, shops in the control of the high-
priestly clan. These markets had a legitimate function,
that, namely, of providing proper animals for the sacrifices. Jesus objected to them for two reasons only: the quite
provincial attitude they reflected as they were conducted
in the Court of the Nations, whereas as Jesus held, quoting
Isa. 56:7, "My house shall be called a house of prayer *for
all the nations.*" How could non-Jews be expected to pray
amid the hubbub of such a bazaar about them? Again, in
the spirit of Jer. 7:11, Jesus says of this part of the Temple, "but you have made it a den of robbers (*lestai*)"
(Mark 11:17). This was surely an objection to the *merce-
nary spirit* that would profit from such *a travesty of true*

religion—commercialization of religion become a fine art!
When the authorities got the point of this challenge and
inquired about it, Jesus' reply in the form of a question
about John the Baptist's credentials was a call to show
some spiritual insight, a challenge to discern the qualifica-
tions of those whom God calls to unique mission.

c. Jesus' preparations for the Last Supper were as elaborate and as carefully planned as those relating to his
entry to Jerusalem. In the East, it is the women who carry
water jars on their heads as they go back and forth to the
village well; Jesus' arrangement that "a man carrying a jar
of water" should meet his emissaries (Mark 14:13) was,
therefore, exceptional and there could be no mistake.
Then, too, Jesus, as before, had arranged the matter of
passwords (v. 14). All this secrecy was essential because
of the traitor (Judas) in the midst of the group of disciples. If the suggestion of deriving Iscariot from the Latin
sicarius (dagger man, assassin) is right, then it is likely
that Judas' motive was one of drawing his Master over
into the Zealot camp, of inducing him to become a Zealot
Messiah of the very sort that Jesus had already spurned
becoming (Matt. 4:8-9). In any case, Jesus wishes to
complete his training of his disciples to face the ordeal
that he sees approaching, a period of testing of such a
character that he can exclaim of it, "Let him who has no
sword sell his mantle and buy one" (Luke 22:36)! The
words of committal at this supper, then, constitute a
challenge to his disciples on Jesus' part, a challenge to
stand fast in their faith in him and in his insight into the
meaning of all that is to happen.

d. Finally, before both the Sanhedrin and the Roman
governor, Pontius Pilate, it is true to say that, not Jesus,
but the court is on trial. For it is quite likely, one believes,
that here as throughout his ministry Jesus refuses to make

up another man's mind for him in the matter of acceptance of himself. Accordingly, we would suggest that neither before the Sanhedrin nor at the Roman tribunal does
Jesus commit himself by an affirmative reply to the question of whether he is the Messiah or "King of the Jews."

The Gospels vary considerably in the words reported as
from his lips in answer to the high priest's question, "Are
you the Christ, the Son of the Blessed?" (Mark 14:61 f.;
Matt. 26:63 f.; Luke 22:70; John 18:19 ff.). Probably
the reason for this is that Jesus did not give a straightforward reply, but rather answered the question with a
question. In neither Aramaic nor Greek is any change in
order of the words required (as in English), in con-
verting a declarative into an interrogative sentence. For
example, for the English "I am" and "Am I?" Aramaic
would read merely *"Ana na"* both ways, and Greek
similarly *"Ego eimi."* In both these languages the only way
to make the distinction in question is by the intonation of
the voice, and this cannot be indicated in a manuscript!
Jesus' following statement that the high priest would "see
the Son of man sitting at the right hand of Power, and
coming with the clouds of heaven" (Mark 14:62) is open
to more than one interpretation, but in any case it probably means no more than John's statement at John
18:20 f.—the Sanhedrin has the evidence to decide about
Jesus' claims if it wishes to do so, and so far as he is
concerned that is where the matter will have to rest.

The same seems to be Jesus' attitude at the court of Pilate (Mark 15:2; Matt. 27:11; Luke 23:3; John 18:33–
38). The Fourth Evangelist seems to go out of his way to
make this fact plain. As with the Sanhedrin, so with Pilate,
Jesus leaves the matter open as to what he is, whether he
should be called "Messiah," "King of the Jews," or by
some other appellative. He does this, one believes, to chal-

lenge his very judges to declare their faith in him, a faith that hopefully will show some small measure of insight into the nature of the spiritual and moral Kingdom of God whose representative Jesus is for those who can see this.

Such is a mere selection of the incidents of Passion Week and, indeed, of the Gospel materials that may claim to exhibit what the "intention of Jesus" was. One has the feeling of having done less than justice to the view that, for a quarter century, this writer and his colleagues have endeavored to represent in the realm of New Testament studies. If this is so, it will be perhaps for two reasons among others: first, one's realization that much one would say has already been adequately covered in this book as we have dealt with the same or similar views of others working in the field; and secondly, the obvious inability of an author to supply anything like an objective critique of his own views! This writer may perhaps be permitted to close with the suggestion that the reader will find in his chapters "The Inescapable Christ—The 'Spirit of Holiness' " and "The Challenge of the Kingdom—Word and Work" much that has the ring of Bornkamm's splendid chapters entitled respectively "Jesus of Nazareth" and "Jesus Christ," at least he would be happy to think so!

Epilogue
Which Jesus?

As one glances back over the pages of this book, certain facts stand out which this writer hopes his readers, along with him, will find it encouraging to observe. For example, there is the undoubted fact that we have come a long way since the turn of the century. In some respects it may even be said that our advance in Biblical studies compares not too unfavorably with the miraculous advance in scientific fields. Discoveries have been made in the realms of archaeology (Khirbet Qumran, Ugarit, Nag Hamadi, Masada, to mention but a few examples), of language study (again Ugaritic, Palestinian Aramaic, Hellenistic Greek, the Minoan inscriptions), of the Biblical manuscripts (again Qumran and the other *wadis,* the pre-Christian MSS. of parts of the O.T., the Caesarean and other N.T. MSS. of first-class value), and in the more elusive fields of psychology and related subjects—all of which may be said to have revolutionized our understanding of the Biblical text. It is therefore, passé to acclaim the "assured results" of the Biblical and theological scholarship preceding the date A.D. 1900! Many questions before that date considered closed and settled have again, in view of the new knowledge in many fields, been reopened.

Accordingly, it is a matter of great satisfaction to note (as observed before in the Introduction to this book) that the subject of Jesus' person and status is not an "open-and-shut" case. Nor is that of his own self-awareness, nor that of whether we may perchance hope to "know the mind" of the historic Jesus about himself. It is better for the continuance of the Christian faith as an active, dynamic, relevant force in the affairs of mankind, one is constrained to believe, that one who seeks to make common cause with the ongoing "people of God" and the church of Christ should be confronted with a choice among seven views of what Jesus of Nazareth was (and is), than that one be confronted with a "dogma" to the effect that there can be but one such view. As long as people are people, it can only be healthy for the spiritual-ethical tone of God's people that each person make up his own mind about Jesus Christ. It was so, we believe, the historic Jesus confronted the men of his own day; it is and always will be so that he will continue to challenge them in the days down to the end of history.

Appendixes

APPENDIX 1. THE "MESSIAH SECRET"

This phrase, first used by Wrede and Schweitzer, refers to the undoubted fact that the Synoptic Gospels represent Jesus as making a *secret* of his Messiahship. Thus, even as late as Peter's confession, Jesus "charged them to tell no one" about his Messiahship (Mark 8:30), even as "he would not permit the demons to speak, because they knew him" (chs. 1:34; cf. 3:11 f.), and told his disciples to "tell no one what they had seen" at the transfiguration, "until the Son of man should have risen from the dead" (ch. 9:9). See further Matt. 11:25-30‖Luke 10:21 f.; Luke 24:25-27; 44-48. The *problem* these data raise is— whether the Gospels are right in attributing the *secret* to Jesus (so Schweitzer) or to the later church (so Wrede).

APPENDIX 2. THE SAYING AT MATT. 10:23

Schweitzer's argument that "the first postponement" of the Kingdom's coming follows Jesus' error indicated at Matt. 10:23 ("Truly, I say to you, you will not have gone through all the towns of Israel, before the Son of man comes") for many years has seemed to this writer to represent a very shallow bit of Synoptic research. It is generally recognized among scholars that we have several accounts of Jesus' first sending out of "the Twelve" (thus, Matt. 9:35 to 10:16, with vs. 17-23 or even more; Mark 6:6-11; Luke 9:1-5—all of which may or may not depend on one source), and that Luke 10:1-12 (usually entitled "the sending out of the Seventy") exhibits curious similarities in detail to the other three accounts. What has apparently been overlooked is that if the well-attested reading "Seventy-two" rather than "Seventy" is accepted as probably original at Luke 10:1, then we have in this chapter a *doublet,* that is, another account of the sending out of the Twelve, and that Luke's sole account of Seventy (-two) being sent on mission by Jesus simply disappears. Two major arguments in favor of this conclusion may be given.

First, in the Greek (if letters standing for numbers were employed in early MSS. rather than spelling out the numbers "12" and "72," a common practice in Greek as in Latin and other languages) it is to be noted that "12" is iota beta and "72," omicron beta. A slight slip of the pen, then, could easily convert "12" into "72," and Luke would simply be employing a doublet of the sending forth of the Twelve in his tenth chapter, doubtless quite unwittingly on his part!

Secondly, that this is, indeed, what really happened and that *Matt., ch. 10, is following the same source (perhaps Q) which Luke has for his ch. 10,* at the same time admittedly combining elements from the other two accounts above noted, seems to be *proved by coincidences between Matt., ch. 10, and Luke, ch. 10, that do not occur in the other accounts.* Use of a harmony of the Synoptic Gospels will exhibit this in detail. Here will be noted some of the more obvious similarities that cannot be gainsaid. Thus, for "sandals," Matt. 10:10 and Luke 10:4 read *hypodemata* (Mark 6:9 having rather *sandalia*); Matt. 10:10 and Luke 10:7 have "for the laborer deserves his food," a saying lacking elsewhere; Matt. 10:13 and Luke 10:6 have essentially the same reference to one's "peace" returning to one, a saying not found in Mark; for "dust," Matt. 10:14 and Luke 9:5 and 10:11 employ *koniorton,* while Mark 6:11 has rater *choun;* finally, Matt. 10:15 and Luke 10:12 (only) have the saying about Sodom (and Gomorrah in Matt. only). It is perhaps also significant that the saying about the disciples being sent "as sheep in the midst of wolves" opens this passage in Luke 10:3 and closes the first section of it in Matt. 10:16, being omitted in the other accounts.

If, then, *we may conclude that Matt., ch. 10, and Luke, ch. 10, are following in part the same source,* surely it becomes *significant that at two points in the discourse, Jesus in Luke (ch. 10:9 and 11) refers to the fact that "the kingdom of God has come near," whereas in Matt. (ch. 10:7) an equivalent statement is made but once.* Accordingly, we are constrained to look round in Matthew's chapter to discover whether some *equivalent* for Luke's second statement of the Kingdom's nearness does not appear. And what we discover is that, after making the insertion about the lot of the disciples under persecution (a section found in substance in the eschatological discourse at Mark 13:9-13 and Luke 21:12-19), *Matthew appears to return to the source he has been following jointly with Luke, ch. 10,* and to *insert at v. 23 the equivalent of Luke's second reference to the near approach of the Kingdom* ("You will not have gone through all the towns of Israel, before the Son of man comes"). As *elsewhere Matthew equates the coming of the Kingdom with that of the Son of*

Man (see Matt.16:28 as compared with the same saying at Mark 9:1 and Luke 9:27), certainly it may be so understood at Matt. 10:23. *In this case, Matt. 10:23 contains nothing new as compared with the other accounts—Jesus here as elsewhere will be merely affirming that in himself, his labors and those of his disciples, the Kingdom of God has drawn nigh, and Schweitzer's "postponement" may be summarily dismissed as a bad piece of exegesis!*

Appendix 3. The Nature of Form Criticism

In a short résumé such as this book represents, one cannot give space to a discussion of Gospel "sources" (generally indicated by the letters Q, M, L, and Mark, the Gospel conceived as substantially a source in its present form of the later Matthew and Luke). However, a short statement relative to *Formgeschichte,* or the development during the period of oral tradition of the series of narrative and teaching passages which one finds in the completed Gospels, is in order. Among numerous English works that may be consulted, the following are of special merit: Rudolf Bultmann's *The History of the Synoptic Tradition* (1963, tr. by John Marsh from the 3d rev. German ed.); Martin Dibelius' *From Tradition to Gospel* (1935, tr. by Bertram L. Woolf from the 2d rev. German ed.); and Vincent Taylor's *The Formation of the Gospel Tradition* (1933).

Employing for the most part Taylor's terms which appear not to beg any questions, as is frequently done in most works including the other two above mentioned, the scholar in the field of form criticism groups all the materials in the Gospels (particularly of the Synoptics, but to a degree also of John) under the following heads:

1. *Pronouncement Stories* or *Apophthegmata*. These are narratives whose whole purpose is to enshrine and transmit a saying of Jesus on some important issue, details of time, person, and place being eliminated or forgotten; examples: fasting (Mark 2:18 ff.), cornfield incident (vs. 23 ff.), tribute money (ch. 12:13 ff.), and the like.

2. *Miracle Stories*. These are short narratives whose intent is, as the term implies, to transmit an account of one or other of Jesus' "mighty works," such as the man with an unclean spirit (Mark 1:21-27), the feeding of the five thousand (ch. 6:34-44), the epileptic boy (ch. 9: 14-29), etc.

3. *Sayings and Parables*. This category includes a large part of the teaching attributed in the Gospels to Jesus— aphorisms, proverbs, poetry, and parables.

4. *Stories About Jesus, Legends, Myths*. This is a convenient "dumping ground" for materials not assignable to any other form; it includes such stories as the infancy narratives, Peter's confession, the transfiguration, the request of James and John. Generally speaking the passion and resurrection narratives are studied by form critics in a category by themselves, though it is recognized that these narratives contain materials assignable to the other categories.

The small space allotted here for criticism of the work of the form critics permits of but a mere few observations that have accumulated during a period of almost forty years of reading and teaching in the field. These must suffice:

1. *Pronouncements and Miracle Stories*. Here one believes the form critics are on firm ground; for in these stories, as is obvious, everything gives way for the "saying" of Jesus or the "mighty work"—all else is secondary, merely supplying embellishment or background. However,

to say this is neither (a) to make a judgment as to the historicity of the event, nor (b) to subscribe to a particular *Sitz im Leben* for the story, nor again (c) to utter a judgment relative to the period of time necessary to round out such a story, nor even (d) to suggest that it was rounded out in the course of transmission from storyteller to storyteller and the like. All these stories might very well represent the established "form" given them by a single evangelist or disciple deliberately eliminating all but the important point(s) he wished to make   r does absence or presence of detail relative to persons, places, and times speak either in favor of or against their historicity. This writer spent a "camping season" of four months in 1924-1925 in a district of Northern India and during that season preached in over three hundred and fifty towns and villages and conducted scores of interviews; he also kept a complete file of places, persons, and dates—later destroying these. Most of his memory of such details has faded during the past forty-five years. But there are a half-dozen names of persons and places which, for one reason and another, he is still prepared to take oath relative to his accurate memory. Such were Jairus, Bartimeus, Mary of Magdala, Cana, and the like, in the Gospels.

2. *Story Parables and Sayings*. These are in quite a different category from the two types of stories just mentioned so far as the subject of credibility is concerned. Jesus, we may well believe, was the greatest master of the story parable in the Jewish tradition, a master, too, of the shorter *mashal* (aphorism, proverb); certainly there is no a priori reason for thinking otherwise, and the only evidence we possess (that of the Gospels) indicates that he was so. That his disciples should have even memorized his literary creations is, too, in line with the Oriental view-

point in which it is the "living word" that inspires reverence, not as in the West, where a thing must be "down in black and white" to be acceptable. Form critics rather generally have tended to be far too Occidental in their point of view. The *hafiz* found all over the Semitic (Arabic) world today is often enough a simple-minded believer who has made of himself a living manuscript of the Arabic *Qoran,* that if all other MSS. perish he may repeat the sacred scripture of his people from beginning to end. Even the Aryan shares this type of expertise in India, where the *Vedas* were passed down with the utmost accuracy by means of "oral tradition" alone for some 3400 years—that is, from around 1500 B.C. to A.D. 1800, when Sir William Jones of the High Court in Calcutta persuaded certain pandits to write out for him (for the first time in history) the Sanskrit scriptures (see Stuart Piggott, *Prehistoric India,* 1950, p. 253).

3. *Stories About Jesus, Legends, Myths.* These, together with the passion and resurrection narratives, require to be examined each for its own sake. Suffice it here to say with C. C. McCown that "the New Testament . . . still very different from Norse sagas, German fairy tales, Jewish haggadah and midrash, and Hellenistic hero legends and cult myths" (MSRJ-206). And as for *myth,* this writer would like to associate himself with Bornkamm's excellent remarks ending with this sentence: "The history of the Israelite-Jewish religion is marked by a continuous struggle against myth" (BJN-34 f.). It should be added that this struggle carries over from O.T. to N.T. and becomes one of the most marked characteristics of the "prophetic realism" of the church's faith and of its belief in the God of History.

APPENDIX 4. DID GOD GIVE THE HOLY LAND
TO ABRAM AND HIS DESCENDANTS?

The claim that this is so has been held throughout the history of the Hebrew-Jewish tradition and is fundamental to Brandon's thesis. It is repeated again and again as basic to his entire argument (BJZ-63n3). The concept was, he claims, "basic to Yahwism" (BJZ-62).

This view is so widely held among both Jewish and Christian scholars, as well as among the rank and file of both communities, and at the same time met with such derision on the part of skeptics and those who, like Bultmann, are concerned about what the "modern man" may be expected to accept, that the validity of the claim needs to be examined.

If the favorite "either-or" argument of German scholarship is applied to the problem, the alternatives may be stated thus:

either (*a*) God promised to Abram and his descendants the land of Canaan for everlasting possession

or (*b*) the claim is a bit of particularistic nonsense arising among the ethnic group that worshiped "Yahweh" (the national god).

But are these the only possible alternatives to be considered? To employ the terminology and method of procedure used in discussing the Wrede-Schweitzer dilemma in Chapter 1, above, we may ask: Is there, indeed, no *tertium quid?* Are we really tied down to these two alternatives?

This writer suggests that we are not, that there is at least a third possible solution to this problem, perhaps there are more. First, however, let it be said that this writer for one is not impressed by the arguments of those who refuse to hear it stated that it would be immoral for Yahweh to grant Canaan to the Hebrew people when it was already occupied by other peoples! There is something illogical about the statement of one like Brandon (and it is stated in various ways by members of various schools of thought), to the effect that "the conception . . . was basic to Yahwism: that Yahweh had chosen the nation to be his own peculiar people and had given to them the land of Canaan as their home and peculiar possession" (BJZ-62). The statement is illogical because, if Yahweh is the Living God of all the earth, then it follows that "he plays no favorites"; or if he is merely a tribal or national or racial god, then Canaan does not belong to him and he cannot give it away. This seems to be an appropriate use of the "either-or" methodology! It is so because the second alternative runs counter to the Hebrew prophetic point of view; this alternative of the national god (Yahweh) is a creation of modern scholarship and has no standing in the prophetic Scriptures.

The *tertium quid* that one would suggest by way of an answer to the question raised in this appendix may be phrased as follows: *The one true God (known as Yahweh or by any other appropriately defining name) selected Canaan as his base of operations and Abraham and his descendants as his chosen instruments that the knowledge of Him might be disseminated across the face of the earth among all peoples.*

It is contended that this third alternative—(a) makes sense if monotheism is a proper concept, (b) "plays no favorites" among peoples, as Amos long since saw to be basic to a monotheistic faith (Amos 9:7), (c) accords with the golden thread of God's universal saving purpose as declared throughout prophetic Scripture in both Old and New Testaments, and (*d*) may be thought acceptable to the elusive "modern man."

Obviously, it would take a book at least as large as the present small volume to document this thesis from the Scriptures. That it runs counter to much modern scholarly opinion, the writer is well aware, but he is also aware of the fact that a point of view can go along quite comfortably and universally accepted on all hands until someone challenges its truth. He confesses to his determination herewith to challenge this pet theme among both Jews and Christians.

To state but one argument, and this with full knowledge of the numerous difficulties that it raises and the vulnerability involved in it by reason of the problems with which oral and written criticisms deal, that of the *Sitz im Leben* that may be implied, and the like, Is it not remarkable that Abraham is said to have gone through the Land of Canaan, staking out a claim for God (not for himself) at those points where God appeared to him by erecting altars, and that for himself he refused to appear to possess a single square foot of the land for which he did not pay (Gen., ch. 23)? This raises the question, In what sense did Abraham (or alternatively, the prophetic writers of Scripture) believe that God had "given" the land for a "possession" throughout history to himself and his people? If this writer may be so bold as to answer this crucial question, he would say: It was only given as a golden opportunity for service to God and man, that Canaan might become the headquarters of a universal mission; and that as one reads Scripture, one discovers that "election" of the individual or the people is always with a view to such service, never to any immediate returns that may accrue in the experience of the person(s) involved, though that such returns do accrue history records as profoundly true.

DATE DUE

DE 7'71			
OC 29 74			
GAYLORD			PRINTED IN U.S.A.